ТРОЙКА

ТРОЙКА

the TROIKA introduction to Russian letters and sounds

by

Reason A. Goodwin

LH

LEXIK HOUSE Publishers

Cold Spring, New York

Library of Congress Cataloging in Publication Data

Goodwin, Reason A.
ТРОЙКА the TROIKA introduction to Russian letters and sounds.
8006 800425 80-81788

ISBN: 0-936368-00-4 (hardcover)
ISBN: 0-936368-01-2 (softcover)

First Edition

Manufactured in the United States of America

TABLE OF CONTENTS

PREFATORY NOTE

This slight booklet just had to be written because for many years I have been saddened on hearing bright people say they are deterred from learning even a smattering of Russian by "that terrible alphabet." Well, now the alphabet isn't all that terrible. A veil, to be sure, but a veil that is easily rent. I have tried by introducing and discussing the Russian letters in easy stages and by illustrating their use in familiar words to show that the mere use of a different alphabet need not make some acquaintance with Russian forbidding or unattainable. The book does not attempt to teach any of the language, but if it does encourage any of its readers to take up that rewarding study I will be highly gratified.

It is pleasant to acknowledge my gratitude for the labor and devotion of my editor David K. Barnhart and for encouragement and helpful suggestions from a number of associates and consultants who read the manuscript in either an earlier or its present form: Clarence L. Barnhart, Thomas L. Clark (University of Nevada, Las Vegas), John R. Costello (New York University), Sol Steinmetz, Robert Ilson, and Leo V. Malakhovski (Institute of Linguistics, U.S.S.R. Academy of Sciences). If in any detail I have not followed their counsel I have done so, I realize, at my peril.

R.A.G.

LESSON ONE

SOME PRELIMINARIES

1.1

This is a book for people who read English but do not read Russian. It is quite different from a primer for Russian children.

When Russians learn to read they must learn to associate Cyrillic letters with words they speak perfectly well. You are no doubt an old hand at the art of reading English, but I assume you are now setting out to learn a new set of letters that record many unfamiliar sounds in words of a language that is largely unknown to you.

I have tried to isolate and dilute the difficulties by first concentrating on learning the letters that look the most familiar and introducing new letters in stages according to their difficulty. To get a little stock to start with, I give you first the letters of the familiar word *troika* (тройка), which include four familiar ones (т, о, к, and а) and two that warn you of what's ahead: the foolers (р is the Russian *r*) and the new faces (й is the diphthongal *i*, as in English *oil*). After that, the letters are introduced one by one, with remarks about shape or origin or use that I think will interest you and help you remember them. The examples in each chapter use only the new letter and those that have already been paraded before you.

After each new word is an indication of the pronunciation (as for, тро́йка "TROI kuh"; самова́р "suh mah-VAHR"). I have marked the principal accented syllable with an acute accent (´) over the appropriate Cyrillic vowel letter and in the pronunciation with capital letters for the appropriate syllable.

I have made remarks about pronunciation to show, for instance, that Russian "t" is not precisely the same as English "t". For the most part, however, sounds are discussed in relation to the writing system. For example, there are two o's in кокóтка "kah KAWT kuh", but the first stands for the "ah" sound in the English word *father* and the second for "aw" as in English *raw*; this calls for a note on the difference between o's in accented and unaccented syllables. But I want you to be able to read through the book without learning rules; hence, a pronunciation rather than a transliteration is furnished for each example.

The simulated pronunciation of кокóтка "kah KAWT-kuh", as you see, is what is popularly called "phonetic"; it pretends to reproduce a Russian word in letters that evoke English sounds. The main expectation is that it will remind you of what is said in the notes about pronunciation; I hope that, at the very least, it will give you some better idea of how the Russian word sounds than what you would produce directly from the Russian characters. The pronunciation key is in the appendix.

From one of the earliest chapters on, you will find discussion and remarks about "hard" and "soft" consonants. This is fundamental to understanding the writing system as well as the contrast of sounds. I try to make the discussion both meaningful and nontechnical. Nevertheless, it cannot be ducked; we need it to show the difference between words such as брат "BRAHT" 'brother' and брать "BRAHT(Y)" 'to take', and why there are different letters (а and я) for the a's in Шаля́пин "shah LYAH-pyin" or "shi LYAH pyin", the name which we spell *Chaliapin*.

Each citation of an example concludes with a gloss:

кокóтка "kah KAWT kuh" 'cocotte'

As this suggests, the examples do not pretend to be a basic or immediately useful vocabulary—or even a "vocabulary" at all. They are merely demonstrations of the letters. I have hunted for examples that have some ring of familiarity. They include names that have some occurence in English, even though some are relatively uncommon (*Lomonosov*, *Vorkuta*, *Nozdrëv*); Russian words that have come into English (*sputnik*, *troika*, *samovar*, *balalaika*); Russian words that were borrowed from English (*futbol* 'football', *khuligan* 'hooligan', *sport* 'sport'); and words that both Russian and English got from some other source (*literatura* 'literature', *avtomat* 'automaton', *seryëznyi* 'serious').

Where different glosses are possible, I often provide only the one that is similar in form; for example, *komod* 'commode', rather than the more familiar 'chest of drawers'.

I have, of course, used a few unfamiliar native Russian words like брат 'brother' and брать 'to take' when they were handy to illustrate a point.

1.2

Modern Russian is written with an alphabet of 32 letters. Capital and small letters with English equivalents in their conventional order look like this:

А	Б	В	Г	Д	Е	Ж	З	И	Й	К
а	б	в	г	д	е	ж	з	и	й	к
a	b	v	g	d	e,ye	zh	z	i,yi	i(y)	k

Л	М	Н	О	П	Р	С	Т	У	Ф	Х
л	м	н	о	п	р	с	т	у	ф	х
l	m	n	o	p	r	s	t	u	f	kh

Ц	Ч	Ш	Щ	*	*	*	Э	Ю	Я
ц	ч	ш	щ	ъ	ы	ь	э	ю	я
ts	ch	sh	shch	(")	y	(')	e	yu	ya

*The letters ъ, ы, and ь never stand initially in a word. In titles, headlines and similar contexts with all capital letters the forms of these letters are the same as the lower case ones.

A character ё, which is a Russian e pronounced "yaw", is sometimes listed with the alphabet. It is explained in section 8.1.

Here are a few generalities you can easily verify by examining this display:

Most of the small letters have the same shapes as the capitals. It is a little strange to have to think of к, м, and т as "small letters," but when you get to the unfamiliar shapes you will be glad that you do not have to learn two of them for each letter. Where the capital and the small letter have different shapes, the pairing is usually matched by similar shapes in our alphabet: А а, Е е, Р р, У у, or the difference is so slight that no one will be hesitant about the identification: Ф ф. The letter for which two materially different new shapes have to be learned is the second in the alphabet: Б б, corresponding to our *B b*.

Many of the Russian letters have the same shapes as letters in our alphabet, but the ones that usually catch a person's eyes when he looks at a sample of Russian are those that are unlike ours or suggest ours modified in some curious way. The last letter, Я, is often taken for a turned-around R. Some people see the letter ч as an upside-down h, and I have heard students call ы (fifth from the end) "the bee-el letter."

Out of the 32 characters, 20 do not occur in our alphabet. Most of these are not like anything you have seen before, but you may observe that з resembles our script z and is indeed the Russian equivalent of *z*; the mathematical symbol π (pi) will help you identify п, which is the equivalent of our *p*; and г, д, л, and ф will not be utter strangers if you know the Greek letters gamma (Γ), delta (Δ), lambda (Λ), and phi (Φ).

The other twelve include some deceptive ones, for only five can fairly be said to be "the same as" the Latin letters they suggest. Those are а, к, м, о, and т. The Russian е comes pretty close, but much of the time it is better represented by "ye" than identified with our single letter *e*. Six have familiar shapes but are not what they seem: в, н, р, с, у correspond to our v, n, r, s, u; and to represent х we have to use an arbitrary combination *kh*.

The utility of тро́йка for a starter is that it contains four of the "same as" letters and at the same time introduces one of the deceptive forms and one of the utter strangers.

THE LETTERS OF *troika*

2.1

тройка = troika

ТРОЙКА = TROIKA

Instead of juggling all six of these letters right off, let us take a closer look at three of the most familiar ones.

2.2

т = t	Т = T
к = k	К = K
а = a	А = A

The Russian а generally represents an "ah" sound, which in American English we often spell with an *o*.

как "KAHK" 'how'

так "TAHK" 'so'

акт "AHKT" 'act'

такт "TAHKT" 'tact'

The "ah" sound persists if а is the first letter or

if it comes in the syllable just before the one that has the principal accent. Both of those conditions are exemplified by the first а in атáка 'attack'. In other unaccented syllables, а represents the relaxed "neutral" vowel of *a* of *canoe* and the second and third *a*'s of *Canada*. Атáка thus sounds like "ah TAH kuh".

To say that как and так rhyme with English *cock* "kahk" and tick-*tock* "tahk" ignores the subtleties of articulation in which Russian and English speech habits differ. The "t" in Russian is a dental: the tip of the tongue touches the back of the upper teeth (for English "t" it touches the gum ridge above the teeth). Furthermore, both the "t" and the "k" in Russian are unaspirated: they are not followed by the slight puff of breath that characterizes "t" and "k" in English.

2.3

Some examples:

кот "KAWT" 'tomcat'

ток "TAWK" 'current'

кокóтка "kah KAWT kuh" 'cocotte'

óко "AW kuh" 'eye'

какáо "kah KAH aw" 'cocoa'

In accented syllables, о represents an "aw" sound, much like the sound which for speakers of English is the vowel in *hawk* and *raw*.

The "aw" sound does not ordinarily occur in unaccented syllables. When о occurs in an unaccented syllable, it stands for the same sound as а, "ah" at the beginning of a word or in the syllable before the accented syllable, elsewhere "uh", the relaxed vowel heard at the end of *troika*.

"Aw" does occur in unaccented syllables in some

words that Russian got from other languages. Какао, the example used here, is the Russian adaptation of either German *Kakao* or French *cacao*.

Here are some other Russian words you can read without difficulty:

от "AWT" 'from'

тот "TAWT" 'that'

кто "KTAW" 'who'

отка́т "aht KAHT" 'recoil'

като́к "kah TAWK" 'roller'

2.4

р = r	Р = R

ро́тор "RAW tuhr" 'rotor'

та́ра "TAH ruh" 'tare'

а́рка "AHR kuh" 'arch'

тра́ктор "TRAHK tuhr" 'tractor'

торт "TAWRT" 'tort'

ка́рта "KAHR tuh" 'map'

акр "AHKR" 'acre'

тракт "TRAHKT" 'highway'

By history and by convention the Russian р is the letter equivalent to our *r*, as these and many other examples show. The sounds, however, are quite different. The smooth, vowellike "r" of American English is a poor substitute for the Russian "r", which is a slight trill, more like the "r" of Spanish and Italian, or the kind of "r" we parody by writing *veddy* for *very*.

You should not take this use of р in place of *r* as evidence of Russian cantankerousness. It has a well-understood historical basis. The Russian alphabet and ours go back to the Greek, but the times and places of the borrowing were different.

The Russian alphabet is a modification of a Slavic alphabet that was devised in the ninth century on the model of the Greek capital letters. The Greek alphabet at that time had settled down to the shapes we know as the Greek alphabet today. It need be no surprise that the character P (called rho in Greek) is an *r* both in Greek and in Russian.

Our letters go back to a much earlier form of the Greek alphabet. They reflect some fluctuations in shapes and uses of the letters in the hands of the ancient Greeks and some modifications as the letters were adopted successively by the Etruscans and by the Romans. In the early shapes that reached the Romans, the characters for *p* and *r* had come to look rather alike; the Romans settled on P for the first and added the extra stroke that distinguishes the R.

Here are some further examples you can now read without difficulty:

аóрта "ah AWR tuh" 'aorta'

Арарáт "ah rah RAHT" 'Ararat'

катáр "kah TAHR" 'catarrh'

катарáкт "kuh tah RAHKT" 'cataract (of a river)'

катарáкта "kuh tah RAHK tuh" 'cataract (in the eye)'

орáтор "ah RAH tuhr" 'orator'

рококó "raw kaw KAW" 'rococo'

трактáт "trahk TAHT" 'treatise' 'treaty'

The remaining letter in тройка is the one that is thoroughly unfamiliar:

й = i	Й = I

It appears as the second part of diphthongs, such as *ai* in *Nikolai*, *ei* in *Yenisei*, *oi* or *oy* in *Tolstoi* or *Tolstoy*, and *ui* in *Kuibyshev*.

The ой in тро́йка is much like our "oi" diphthong; рой "ROI" 'swarm' sounds like the English name *Roy* (with, of course, the different "r").

ко́йка "KOI kuh" 'cot'

кро́йка "KROI kuh" 'cutting out (of cloth)'

тако́й "tah KOI" 'such'

The diphthong ай is like our "long *i*" in *isle* and *aisle*. We are familiar with Russian examples such as *Nikolai* and *balalaika*. Three words you can read with the diphthong ай are:

рай "RAI" 'paradise'

край "KRAI" 'border'

тарата́йка "tuh rah TAI kuh" 'two-wheeled vehicle'

Occasionally, in borrowed words and foreign names, й represents a "y" sound before a vowel. Two easy examples are:

йота "YAW tuh" 'iota'

Йорк "YAWRK" 'York'

Russian letters have names, just as ours do. Here are those for the six letters in тройка:

т *te* ("TE")

р *er* ("ER")

о *o* ("AW")

й *i kratkoye* ("EE KRAHT kuh yuh"), which means 'short *i*'

к *ka* ("KAH")

а *a* ("AH")

М ("EM"): M

3.1

м = m	М = M

ма́ма "MAH muh" 'mamma'

май "MAI" 'May'

майо́р "mah YAWR" 'major'

Марк "MAHRK" 'Mark'

мат "MAHT" 'mate (in chess)'

ма́рка "MAHR kuh" 'mark'

а́том "AH tuhm" 'atom'

тома́т "tah MAHT" 'tomato'

The only thing strange about this letter is the use of the same form for the capital and for the small letter. Even its name is the same as ours: *em* ("EM"). Some further examples:

Мака́р "mah KAHR" 'Makar, Macarius'

март "MAHRT" 'March'

мото́р "mah TAWR" 'motor'

ром "RAWM" 'rum'

том "TAWM" 'tome'

Тама́ра "tah MAH ruh" 'Tamara'

ом "AWM" 'ohm'

мо́йка "MOI kuh" 'washing'

каймáк "kai MAHK" 'thick cream'

мокро́та "mah KRAW tuh" 'phlegm'

мокротá "muh krah TAH" 'dampness'

аромáт "ah rah MAHT" 'aroma'

3.2

Russian allows combinations of consonants that will strike you as definitely unorthodox or unfair, especially at the beginning of a word. Here are two:

мрáмор "MRAH muhr" 'marble'

мрак "MRAHK" 'darkness'

Both мрáмор and *marble* came from Latin *marmor*, but different things happened to the word on its way to modern Russian and to modern English.

В ("VE"): V

4.1

в = v	В = V

Варва́ра "vahr VAH ruh" 'Barbara'

ва́рвар "VAHR vuhr" 'barbarian'

окта́ва "ahk TAH vuh" 'octave'

трамва́й "trahm VAI" 'streetcar' 'tramway'

What looks like a *b* turns out to be the Russian v. It is called *ve* ("VE"). Since both our *B* and this Russian letter go back to the Greek beta, this looks like a needless complication. The explanation once again is in the time of the borrowings. Our *B* goes back, through Latin, to the Greek beta when beta represented a "b" sound; the *b*'s in *Barbara* and *barbarian* stand for "b" sounds in English and in the corresponding words in Latin and ancient Greek. But there was a sound change in Greek whereby the "b" sound became a "v". That had occurred by the ninth century; it was quite natural that the Slavs took over the letter *B* to represent their "v" sound. When they borrowed Greek words that contained a beta, they pronounced the beta as these later Greeks did—as a "v". That is why Russian has a letter of *B* shape that represents a "v" sound, and why such related words as варвар and *barbarian*, Варвара and *Barbara* are spoken with "v" in Russian and "b" in English.

A few other words in which this letter occurs:

ватт "VAHT" 'watt'

Вайт "VAIT" '(Isle of) Wight'

кварта "KVAHR tuh" 'quart'

квóта "KVAW tuh" 'quota'

трáвма "TRAH vmuh" 'trauma'

Аврóра "ah VRAW ruh" 'Aurora, Avrora'

Авраáм "ah vrah AHM" 'Abraham'

мавр "MAHVR" 'Moor'

Мáвра "MAH vruh" 'Mavra (title of an opera)'

рвóта "RVAW tuh" 'vomiting'

4.2

Sometimes where a в is written, the sound heard is an "f" instead of a "v":

áвтор "AH ftuhr" 'author'

автомáт "ah ftah MAHT" 'automaton'

трáвка "TRAH fkuh" 'grass'

вторóй "ftah ROI" 'second'

This is the work of assimilation, the change of a sound under the influence of another. It is assimilation that makes us say "clipt" although we write *clipped*, and "clubz" although we write *clubs*. What happens is this: the *p* in *clip* is made without vibration of the vocal chords—it is *voiceless*. The sound of *t* is also voiceless. A *d* is normally pronounced with vibrating vocal chords—it is *voiced*; but in *clipped* the *d* becomes a voiceless *t* in accomodation to the voiceless *p*. Assimilation in these English examples is an afterthought: the second of two consonants is affected by the first. In Russian, assimilation is anticipatory: the first consonant adapts itself to the one that follows. If the second is voiceless, the first is also voiceless if Russian sounds allow any choice in the matter: what is written *v* becomes an "f", *d* is pronounced "t", *z* becomes an "s", and so on. Assimilation does not affect *l*, *m*, *n*, and *r*, which stand for voiced sounds that are not paired with any similar voiceless ones.

4.3

There is also a general practice in Russian that where there is a pair of consonants that are alike except that one is voiced and the other voiceless ("v/f, d/t, z/s", and others), the voiced consonant written at the end of a word is replaced in speech by the voiceless one. That is why an "f" is heard where *v* is written in familiar names such as *Chekhov*, *Khrushchev*, and *Molotov*.

Here are some you can read with letters you know:

Ма́рков "MAHR kuhf" 'Markov'

Ко́тов "KAW tuhf" 'Kotov'

Катко́в "kaht KAWF" 'Katkov'

кров "KRAWF" 'roof'

ров "RAWF" 'ditch'

Н ("EN"): N

Н = n	Н = N

но́та "NAW tuh" 'note'

А́нна "AHN nuh" 'Anna' (both n's are pronounced in Russian)

Анто́н "ahn TAWN" 'Anton' 'Anthony'

Рома́нов "rah MAH nuhf" 'Romanov'

You may have a hard time getting used to reading this letter as an *n*, but that is exactly what it is. Its name is *en* ("EN"). It is even connected historically with our *N*, which is also a perfectly good capital *N* in the Greek alphabet. During the centuries when books were written by hand, the Russian scribes let that cross stroke wander a bit. The present shapes of the Russian letters are largely those that were fixed by Peter the Great. Peter found that the H of the Latin alphabet was closer to the n of the first Russian printed books than our *N* would have been, and from that time on, Н has been the Russian *n*.

The "n" sound in Russian, like the "t", is a dental: the tip of the tongue touches the back of the upper teeth rather than the gum ridge as it is in English.

Here are some further examples for reading practice:

но́рма "NAWR muh" 'norm'

нана́йка "nah NAI kuh" 'Nanai woman'

атама́н "ah tah MAHN" 'ataman'

канвá "kahn VAH" 'canvas'

караван "kuh rah VAHN" 'caravan'

контрáкт "kahn TRAHKT" 'contract'

Нáрва "NAHR vuh" 'Narva'

квант "KVAHNT" 'quantum'

кóкон "KAW kuhn" 'cocoon'

конвóй "kahn VOI" 'convoy'

корóна "kah RAW nuh" 'crown'

кран "KRAHN" 'crane'

райóн "rah YAWN" 'raion' 'district'

тон "TAWN" 'tone'

тóнна "TAWN nuh" 'ton'

трон "TRAWN" 'throne'

5.2

танк "TAHN|K" 'tank'

ворóнка "vah RAWN kuh" 'funnel'

кóнка "KAWN kuh" 'horsecar'

The point of these examples is that Russian does not have the "ng" sound that we have before *k* in *tank* and before *g* in *anger*. An Н before a Russian *k* or *g* is pronounced as a dental "n" just as it is when other letters follow it.

Some pairs which will help you practice this follow:

ра́на "RAH nuh" 'wound'
ра́нка "RAHN kuh" 'slight wound'

корóна "kah RAW nuh" 'crown'
корóнка "kah RAWN kuh" 'crown (of a tooth)'

картóн "kahr TAWN" 'cardboard'
картóнка "kahr TAWN kuh" 'cardboard box'

С ("ES"): S

6.1

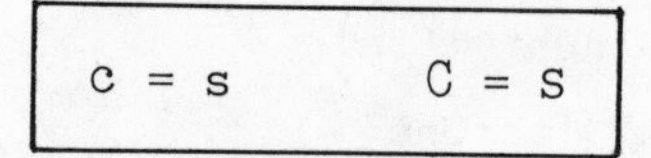

с = s   С = S

самова́р "suh mah VAHR" 'samovar'

СССР "ES ES ES ER" 'USSR'

ТАСС "TAHS" 'TASS'

Москва́ "mah SKVAH" 'Moscow'

ко́смос "KAW smuhs" 'cosmos'

космона́вт "kuh smah NAHFT" 'cosmonaut'

астрона́вт "ah strah NAHFT" 'astronaut'

This is *es* ("ES"), the Russian *s*.

As a memory jogger, it is helpful to recall that our *c* sometimes represents an "s" sound (*cent, civil, cyanide*). Actually, there is no historical connection between the Russian letter and what seems to be an equivalent letter of ours. The Russian с is from a form of the Greek sigma (Σ). Our *c* is from gamma; that is easier to realize when you recall that *c* also very often represents a "k" sound.

Here are some more examples:

Сама́ра "sah MAH ruh" 'Samara'

сона́та "sah NAH tuh" 'sonata'

Сара́тов "sah RAH tuhf" 'Saratov'

сатана́ "suh tah NAH" 'Satan'

Амо́с "ah MAWS" 'Amos'

Акса́ков "ah KSAH kuhf" 'Aksakov'

а́стра "AH struh" 'aster (flower)'

ка́ста "KAH stuh" 'caste'

квас "KVAHS" 'kvass' 'quass' (sour drink)

кокс "KAWKS" 'coke'

Ко́рсаков "KAWR suh kuhf" 'Korsakov'

ма́ска "MAH skuh" 'mask'

ма́сса "MAHS suh" 'mass'

нос "NAWS" 'nose'

Омск "AWMSK" 'Omsk'

Томск "TAWMSK" 'Tomsk'

Росто́в "rah STAWF" 'Rostov'

Тара́с "tah RAHS" 'Taras'

таранта́с "tuh rahn TAHS" 'tarantass'

ост "AWST" 'east'

тост "TAWST" 'toast'

астроно́м "ah strah NAWM" 'astronomer'

станс "STAHNS" 'stanza'

Words with the suffix -ство:

а́вторство "AH ftuhr stvuh" 'authorship'

масо́нство "mah SAWN stvuh" 'freemasonry'

мотовство́ "muh tahf STVAW" 'wastefulness'

сватовство́ "svuh tahf STVAW" 'matchmaking'

скотство́ "skaht STVAW" 'brutality'

сво́йство "SVOI stvuh" 'virtue' 'property'

свойство́ "svai STVAW" 'relationship (by marriage)'

Е ("YE"): E or YE

7.1

е = e, ye   Е = E, Ye

Е́ва "YE vuh" 'Eve'

Ката́ев "kah TAH yif" 'Katayev'

нет "NYET" 'no'

сове́т "sah VYET" 'Soviet'

теа́тр "tyi AHTR" 'theater'

This letter has a familiar and easy look, but it is loaded with trouble. It is called *ye* ("YE"). It is historically connected with our *e*, and sometimes it represents a single sound much like the *e* in *met*. Often, however, it stands for a blend of two sounds, as it does in Ева and Катаев above. Furthermore, the nature of the sound or sounds it represents varies between accented and unaccented syllables, as "YE vuh" and "kah TAH yif" suggest. These examples do not exhaust the difficulties connected with this innocent-looking letter, but it is enough to suggest that we attack the problems peicemeal.

7.2

Éва "YE vuh" 'Eve'

ем "YEM" 'eat' (in the phrase 'I eat')

ест "YEST" 'eats'

At the beginning of a syllable, the Russian е is conveniently transliterated by *ye*. The pronunciation, in stressed syllables, is generally equivalent to the beginning of *yet* and *yesterday*.

Examples within a word are not easy to cite, within the limits of the Russian letters you have been exposed to. One that will do is a word meaning 'will eat' (with various special twists of meaning): наéст "nah YEST".

7.3

нет "NYET" 'no'

тéма "TYE muh" 'theme'

крокéт "krah KYET" 'croquet'

комéта "kah MYE tuh" 'comet'

совéт "sah VYET" 'Soviet'

карéта "kah RYE tuh" 'carriage'

сéкта "SYEK tuh" 'sect'

арéна "ah RYE nuh" 'arena'

вест "VYEST" 'west wind'

конвéрт "kahn VYERT" 'envelope'

When е follows a consonant, it can also be said to stand for "ye", as the simulated pronunciations in these examples suggest—but in a very special way. What we cannot show in a transcription based on English is that the "y" sound here loses its identity and is blended with the consonant that is written before it.

That means that the other consonant is articulated with the tongue in or near the position it takes for making a "y" sound. Fortunately, there is a trick by which you can make yourself do this, well enough for our immediate purposes, without technical phonetic directions: put the tip of your tongue back of your lower teeth and hold it there or try to hold it there while you undertake to pronounce the consonant suggested by the other letter. The desired effect is to bunch the tongue in the front of the mouth, with much of the front of it raised toward the hard palate, as if you were simultaneously making a "y" sound.

This exercise is easier and more effective with some consonants than with others. Easiest and best are very likely the "ny" and "ty" in нет and тема. Hardest is probably the "ry" in карета; you cannot hold the tip of your tongue down for a trill; but starting from that position does help produce an "r" with the top of the tongue lifted toward the hard palate. With any of them you should come closer to the Russian pronunciation than you would by saying what "NYET" and "TYE-" and so on suggest in English sounds. Those spellings do show what (until we learn better) we think we hear when the Russian words are spoken. They represent the pronunciation well enough if you will just remember that "ny" or "ty" or the like is a combination rather than a sequence; if you hear a fleeting suggestion of a "y" sound it is just a grace note in the transition to the following vowel.

None of these combined sounds if pronounced as sequence of plain consonant and "y" satisfies a Russian ear. The greatest violence is done probably by "sy" pronounced in such a fashion. The Russian sound is marked by a much sharper hiss than the usual "s" sound; the plain "s" and full "y" sound is a woefully unfaithful substitute.

You may think this is too much fussing over a detail that is hard to explain and hard to grasp. The importance of understanding that the consonant and the "y" are a combination rather than a sequence will appear as we go along.

These "y"-blended sounds are traditionally called "soft" consonants. The term will not (in any way of which I am aware) help you grasp their nature or their acoustic effect. Actually, "sharp" is a better physical analogy, as I have already suggested for the soft "s".

Nevertheless, "soft" is a term established by long use. So is the term "hard" consonants which, by contrast, names the consonants that do not have the "y" amalgam.

The next point is that most Russian consonants occur in pairs. One in each pair is hard (plain, normal from our point of view), the other soft (articulated as if simultaneously making a "y" sound). A notable and labor-saving feature of the writing system is that the same letter is made to do for the hard and for the soft consonant in each pair. This works because there are other ways of indicating the hardness or the softness of a consonant. The letter е is one of the indicators: the consonant before it is soft (unless that consonant is one of a very few that are always hard, so that there is no choice to be made). The letters in нет, one by one, stand for *n-ye-t*, but the sounds are "ny-e-t". Similarly, тема has four letters: *t-ye-m-a*, but the four sounds are "ty-e-m-a".

In transliterating Russian into our alphabet, there is much uncertainty over the representation of this letter е. It works well for general purposes to use simply *e* rather than *ye*, after a consonant. *Mendeleyev* is better than "Myendyelyeyev", and *Alekseyev* than "Alyeksyeyev", and *Turgenev* than "Turgyenyev". No one need be fooled, for anyone who wants to pronounce any of these names *à la russe* should know that the consonants before the *e*'s in all of them are soft.

Here are some further examples:

манéра "mah NYE ruh" 'manner'

текст "TYEKST" 'text'

оркéстр "ahr KYESTR" 'orchestra'

мéтр "MYETR" 'meter'

момéнт "mah MYENT" 'moment'

Вéра "VYE ruh" 'Vera'

Вéна "VYE nuh" 'Vienna'

крем "KRYEM" 'cream'

сéктор "SYEK tuhr" 'sector'

кокéтка "kah KYET kuh" 'flirt'

кокéтство "kah KYET stvuh" 'flirtation'

7.4

Катáев "kah TAH yif" 'Katayev'

Невá "nyi VAH" 'Neva'

теáтр "tyi AHTR" 'theater'

океáн "ah kyi AHN" 'ocean'

метрó "myi TRAW" 'Metro' 'subway'

ветерáн "vyi tyi RAHN" 'veteran'

ресторáн "ryi stah RAHN" 'restaurant'

секрéт "syi KRYET" 'secret'

"Ye" or "e" after a soft consonant is usually confined to accented syllables. It may be heard in unaccented syllables in deliberate speech or in words pronounced alone. In normal speech it is replaced by "yi" or "i" in which the vowel may be compared either to what we call a "short i" or to a relaxed "ee"; it sometimes suggests what we spell with *i* in *comic* or *punish*, and sometimes the *i* in *piano* or *yogi*. When "yi" is written after a consonant, in the pronunciations, it approximates this relaxed "i" or "ee" following a soft consonant.

Here are a few more examples:

в мáе "VMAH yi" 'in May'

террáса "tyi RAH suh" 'terrace'

термóметр "tyir MAW myitr" 'thermometer'

мáстер "MAH styir" 'master'

тáнкер "TAHN kyir" 'tanker'

7.5

In certain grammatical functions, an unaccented е at the end of a word behaves like any other unaccented е, as the example в мае in the last section was meant to suggest. In some uses, however, an unaccented е at the end of a word represents "yuh", or "a" after a soft consononant, in which the vowel is like the *a* in *soda*.

Some examples are:

мóре "MAW ryuh" 'sea'

нóвое "NAW vuh yuh" 'new'

Крáсное мóре "KRAH snuh yuh MAW ryuh" 'the Red Sea'

7.6

ей "YEI" 'her'

моéй "mah YEI" 'my'

Матвéй "mah TVYEI" 'Matvei (Matthew)'

Еврéй "yi VRYEI" 'Jew'

крéйсер "KRYEI syir" 'cruiser'

Ей is "yei", or "ei" after a soft consonant. The diphthong is much the same as what we spell with *ei* in *eight*, *ey* in *they*, *ay* in *play*.

REVIEW

The following will help you review *Lesson Seven*:

ракéта "rah KYE tuh" 'rocket'

сквер "SKVYER" 'square' 'public garden'

кáмера "KAH myi ruh" 'camera'

теорéма "tyi ah RYE muh" 'theorem'

Еврéйка "yi VRYEI kuh" 'Jewess'

Ë: THE MYSTERY OF FEDOR/FËDOR/FYODOR/FIODOR

8.1

актер *or* актёр "ahk TYAWR" 'actor'

тетка *or* тётка "TYAWT kuh" 'aunt'

Семен *or* Семён "syi MYAWN" 'Semën, Semyon (Simeon)'

Семенов *or* Семёнов "syi MYAW nuhf" 'Semënov, Semyonov'

One of the seemingly capricious difficulties of Russian spelling is that the letter е sometimes represents not "YE" but "YAW".

The Russians sometimes indicate this pronunciation by writing the е with a dieresis, thus: ё. This is done customarily in reference books and in books for non-Russians. Sometimes it is followed in transliterating Russian names, as in *Fëdor* for *Fedor* "FYAW duhr" or *Potëmkin* for *Potemkin* "pah TYAWM kyin".

Russian names that contain this kind of a е (ё) often appear in English in spellings that undertake to reproduce the sounds rather than the letters. That is why you will find *Fedor*, *Fëdor*, *Fyodor*, or *Fiodor* to represent the same Russian name. *Potiomkin* and *Potyomkin* occur as variants of *Potemkin* or *Potëmkin*. Other examples are *Petr/Pëtr/Pyotr/Piotr*; *Alesha/Alësha/Alyosha*; *Nozdrev/Nozdrëv/Nozdryoff*; *Orel/Orël/Oryol*.

A handy thing about the use of ё to indicate this pronunciation is that it shows where the accent is; "YAW" occurs only in accented syllables.

И ("EE"): I

15

9.1

И = i   И = I

и "EE" 'and' 'also'

Искра "EE skruh" 'Iskra' ('The Spark')

Истра "EE struh" 'Istra'

Ирма "EER muh" 'Irma'

Каир "kah EER" 'Cairo'

Раиса "rah EE suh" 'Raissa'

кокаин "kuh kah EEN" 'cocaine'

This is the letter for *i* as a full vowel. Its name is *i* ("EE"), and it represents an "ee" sound, as our *i* does in such words as *machine* and *police*.

The letter came from the Greek eta (H), which had come to be pronounced "ee" by the time the Slavic alphabet was patterned upon the Greek in the ninth century. The direction of the cross stroke is the result of scribal habits which ended in fixing this shape И for *i* while the shape H became the Russian *n*.

The *i kratkoye* 'short *i*' (Й) which you have already met as the *i* part of a diphthong originated as a modification of this letter.

9.2

Ни́на "NYEE nuh" 'Nina'

сати́ра "sah TYEE ruh" 'satire'

Ки́ев "KYEE yif" 'Kiev'

ми́на "MYEE nuh" 'mine'

Ви́ктор "VYEEK tuhr" 'Victor'

Екатери́на "yi kuh tyi RYEE nuh" 'Catherine'

Макси́м "mah KSYEEM" 'Maxim'

И, like е, is one of the letters that shows that the preceding consonant is soft. That is, after a consonant, и can be said to represent "yee", if the "y" is understood as being combined with the consonant. (If you want to reread what was said about this before, go back to section 7.3).

Other examples:

сати́н "sah TYEEN" 'sateen'

арти́ст "ahr TYEEST" 'artist'

Константи́н "kuhn stahn TYEEN" 'Constantine'

рис "RYEES" 'rice'

риск "RYEESK" 'risk'

ритм "RYEETM" 'rhythm'

Си́монов "SYEE muh muhf" 'Simonov'

касси́р "kahs SYEER" 'cashier'

9.3

Ива́н "ee VAHN" 'Ivan' 'John'

Моисе́й "mah ee SYEI" 'Moses'

кино́ "kyee NAW" 'cinema'

Ники́та "nyee KYEE tuh" 'Nikita'

ви́ски "VYEE skyee" 'whiskey'

сто́ик "STAW ik" 'stoic'

ко́мик "KAW myik" 'comic'

матема́тика "muh tyi MAH tyi kuh" 'mathematics'

The vowel represented by и in unaccented syllables is not as tense as the "ee" vowel in accented syllables. It can be compared sometimes to a relaxed "ee" and sometimes to our "short *i*". That is about what was said in section 7.5 about е in unaccented syllables. For some speakers of Russian, the distinction between the sounds of е and и vanishes in unaccented syllables. For others, the sounds are at least so close that when young Russians learn to write they need some rules and a lot of training in the correct spelling of words that contain this е or и in unaccented positions.

More examples for reading practice:

ико́на "ee KAW nuh" 'icon'

Ири́на "ee RYEE nuh" 'Irene'

Тито́в "tyee TAWF" 'Titov'

витами́н "vyee tah MYEEN" 'vitamin'

систе́ма "syee STYE muh" 'system'

Енисе́й "yi nyee SYEI" 'Yenisei'

кри́тик "KRYEE tyik" 'critic'

и́рис "EE ryis" 'iris'

анто́ним "ahn TAW nyim" 'antonym'

тата́рин "tah TAH ryin" 'Tatar'

9.4

Russian also has a diphthong ий which appears, for example, in Новороссийск "nuh vuh rah SYEESK" 'Novorossiisk'. Our "ee" in words such as *see* and *tree* is usually a diphthong and hence more like Russian ий than the Russian и, which is a pure vowel; one of our tasks in learning to speak Russian well is to train ourselves to pronounce и without the diphthongal ending of our "ee".

The place where you will see ий most often is in the unaccented syllable -ский *-skii*. This is a suffix that forms adjectives; it is the original of the *-sky* or *-ski* you have seen in many Russian names. There is some variation in the way Russians pronounce this syllable. One of the pronunciations is reasonably close in acoustic effect to the way we pronounce *-sky* in *pesky* and *Stravinsky*, with no softening of the "k".

Here are some examples using letters you know:

америка́нский "ah myi ryee KAHN ski" 'American'

австри́йский "ah FSTRYEE ski" 'Austrian'

Страви́нский "strah VYEEN ski" 'Stravinsky'

Ри́мский "RYEEM ski" 'Rimsky'

Остро́вский "ah STRAWF ski" 'Ostrovsky'

9.5

Аме́рика "ah MYEI ryi kuh" 'America'

косме́тика "kah SMYEI tyi kuh" 'cosmetics'

Каре́нина "kah RYEI nyi nuh" 'Karenina'

Есе́нин "yi SYEI nyin" 'Yesenin' 'Essenin'

Каве́рин "kah VYEI ryin" 'Kaverin'

Моисе́ев "mah ee SYEI yif" 'Moisseyev'

When е is followed by a soft consonant its pronunciation is closer to what we call a "long *a*" (as in *mate*) than to "e" (as in *met*). This is one of the incidental effects of the movement of the tongue into and out of the "y" position; a vowel before or after a soft consonant is formed with the tongue a little higher and a little farther forward than it is otherwise; this effect is greatest when the vowel comes between two soft consonants, as in these examples. The sound which I have here compared to our "ei" is not, of course, as long as the diphthong in ей which we also have to compare with "ei" (section 7.6).

Review

кварти́ра "kvahr TYEE ruh" 'apartment'

кварти́рка "kvahr TYEER kuh" 'small apartment'

три "TRYEE" 'three'

три́о "TRYEE aw" 'trio'

три́ста "TRYEE stuh" 'three hundred'

антиква́р "ahn tyee KVAHR" 'antiquarian'

мотори́ст "muh tah RYEEST" 'motor mechanic'

кри́тика "KRYEE tyi kuh" 'criticism'

ми́мик "MYEE myik" 'mimic'

инсти́нкт "een STYEEN|KT" 'instinct'

ки́рка "KYEER kuh" 'Lutheran Church'

кирка́ "kyeer KAH" 'pick'

ки́ска "KYEE skuh" 'kitty'

киста́ "kyee STAH" 'cyst'

квартира́нт "kvuhr tyee RAHNT" 'lodger'

квартирме́йстер "kvuhr tyeer MYEI styir" 'quarter-master'

евре́йский "yi VRYEI ski" 'Jewish'

океа́нский "ah kyi AHN ski" 'oceanic'

сове́тский "sah VYET ski" 'Soviet'

тре́тий "TRYEI tyi" 'third'

У ("OO"): U

10.1

У = u	У = U

урáн "oo RAHN" 'uranium'

Урáн "oo RAHN" 'Uranus'

рýсский "ROO ski" 'Russian'

Мýрманск "MOOR muhnsk" 'Murmansk'

Воркутá "vuhr koo TAH" 'Vorkuta'

сóус "SAW oos" 'sauce'

У is the equivalent of *u* in our alphabet, and like our *u* in *rule* and *Luke* represents an "oo" sound. The sound supplies the name of the letter: *u* ("OO").

It came from the Greek upsilon (Υ). The modern form is a simplification of a character that was more like *OY*, which—in capital letters—is the Greek *ou*, spelling an "oo" sound. Both Уран and *Uranus* go back (ours through Latin) to Greek *ouranós*.

Some more words you can read with this letter:

ýрна "OOR nuh" 'urn'

курс "KOORS" 'course'

кнут "KNOOT" 'knout'

Иркýтск "eer KOOTSK" 'Irkutsk'

сýмма "SOOM muh" 'sum'

Сумаро́ков "soo mah RAW kuhf" 'Sumarokov'

Вну́ково "VNOO kuh vuh" 'Vnukovo'

нату́ра "nah TOO ruh" 'nature'

структу́ра "strook TOO ruh" 'structure'

мину́та "myee NOO tuh" 'minute'

Аму́р "ah MOOR" 'Amur'

аму́р "ah MOOR" 'Cupid' 'amour'

ка́ктус "KAHK toos" 'cactus'

ко́нус "KAW noos" 'cone'

ва́куум "VAH koo oom" 'vacuum'

инструме́нт "een stroo MYENT" 'instrument'

коммуни́ст "kuhm moo NYEEST" 'communist'

ко́нтур "KAWN toor" 'contour'

миксту́ра "myeek STOO ruh" 'mixture'

рути́на "roo TYEE nuh" 'routine'

тури́ст "too RYEEST" 'tourist'

умо́ра "oo MAW ruh" 'funny thing'

Интури́ст "een too RYEEST" 'Intourist'

Х ("KHAH"): KH

17

11.1

х = kh	Х = Kh

ах! "AKH!" (German) 'ach!'

Óйстрах "OI strukh" 'Oistrakh'

хан "KHAHN" 'khan'

хáки "KHAH kyee" 'khaki'

Стахáнов "stah KHAH nuhf" 'Stakhanov'

We do not have a "kh" sound in English, although "h" has some resemblance to it. It is made with the tongue raised in the back of the mouth toward the position for making a "k" but with the breath passing through instead of being blocked as it is for a "k" sound. You may have learned to say such a sound in German (as in Ba*ch*) or in Spanish (as in Mé*x*ico, "ME hee ko").

Since we do not have the sound we naturally have no established way of spelling it. In Russian words we conventionally represent the letter х by *kh*, as in *Chekhov*, *Khrushchev*, and *kolkhoz*.

The letter's name is *kha* ("KHAH").

It is from the Greek chi (X). It was a natural borrowing in Slavic, for the Greek chi also stands for a "kh" sound. When the Romans borrowed Greek words containing this letter, they wrote *ch* and pronounced simply "k". That is what we do today in words of Greek origin (*chorus*, *character*, and many others). The letter chi has a curious survival in *Xmas*, where *X* stands for the first letter in the Greek name for Christ.

You will often find Х in Russian corresponding to *ch* in English, in words from Greek.

Here are some examples:

хор "KHAWR" 'chorus'

ха́ос "KHAH aws" *or* хао́с "khah AWS" 'chaos'

хара́ктер "khah RAHK tyir" 'character'

мона́рх "mah NAHRKH" 'monarch'

е́внух "YE vnookh" 'eunuch'

меха́ник "myi KHAH nyik" 'mechanic'

Са́хар "SAH khuhr" 'sugar' also has a Х that goes back to a Greek chi (Χ), but in this instance we got our word through another channel.

Sometimes an *h* in another language becomes a Х when the word is adopted in Russian:

хо́ра "KHAW ruh" 'hora'

хокке́й "khah KYEI" 'hockey'

Саха́ра "sah KHAH ruh" 'Sahara'

11.2

хи́на "KHYEE nuh" 'quinine'

хини́н "khyee NYEEN" (another word for) 'quinine'

архи́в "ahr KHYEEV" 'archives'

схе́ма "SKHYE muh" 'scheme'

хе́рес "KHYEI ryis" 'sherry'

That last one is an oddity. Both the Russian херес and the English *sherry* come from *Xeres*, pronounced something like "SHEI res", an old form of the Spanish place name that is now written *Jerez*. Russian writing still shows the old initial letter, and English preserves the old initial sound.

Before е *or* и, a х stands for a "kh" combined with a "y" (section 7.3). The movement of the tongue toward a "y" position causes the articulation to be made somewhat farther forward than it otherwise is.

A few more examples with soft "kh":

хи́мик "KHYEE myik" 'chemist'

Хива́ "khyee VAH" 'Khiva'

химе́ра "khyee MYE ruh" 'chimera'

архите́ктор "ahr khyee TYEK tuhr" 'architect'

архитекту́ра "ahr khyee tyik TOO ruh" 'architecture'

херуви́м "khyi roo VYEEM" 'cherubim'

Херсо́н "khyir SAWN" 'Kherson'

Хера́сков "khyi RAH skuhf" 'Kheraskov'

З("ZE"): Z

12.1

з = z	З = Z

зóна "ZAW nuh" 'zone'

Захáр "zah KHAR" 'Zakhar (Zachary)'

казáк "kah ZAHK" 'Cossack'

Азóв "ah ZAWF" 'Azov'

Карамáзов "kuh rah MAH zuhf" 'Karamazov'

This is one of the letters that have shapes that do not occur in our printed alphabet. It is the Russian letter for z, and it does at least resemble the script form of our z. It is called *ze* ("ZE").

Some further examples:

Зосúма "zah SYEE muh" 'Zosima'

вáза "VAH zuh" 'vase'

вúза "VYEE zuh" 'visa'

рóза "RAW zuh" 'rose'

вискóза "vyee SKAW zuh" 'viscose' 'rayon'

Тéмза "TYEM zuh" 'Thames'

Кутýзов "koo TOO zuhf" 'Kutuzov'

саркáзм "sahr KAHZM" 'sarcasm'

коммунúзм "kuhm moo NYEEZM" 'Communism'

извéстие "ee ZVYEI styi yuh" 'news' 'information'

12.2

ЗИС "ZYEES" 'ZIS' (a Russian car)

зени́т "zyi NYEET" 'zenith'

розе́тка "rah ZYET kuh" 'rosette'

музе́й "moo ZYEI" 'museum'

Карамзи́н "kuh rahm ZYEEN" 'Karamzin'

кри́зис "KRYEE zyis" 'crisis'

транзи́т "trahn ZYEET" 'transit'

оа́зис "aw AH zyis" 'oasis'

кузи́на "koo ZYEE nuh" 'cousine'

рези́на "ryi ZYEE nuh" 'rubber'

The soft "z" (in зе and зи in these examples) is spoken with the tongue bunched in the front of the mouth (section 7.3); the buzz is rather sharper than the plain "z"; "zy" is a reminder of this but a plain "z" followed by a "y" sound would be a quite inadequate substitute.

12.3

ска́зка "SKAH skuh" 'tale'

Кавка́з "kah FKAHS" 'Caucasus'

ука́з "oo KAHS" 'ukase'

марки́з "mahr KYEES" 'marquis'

карни́з "kahr NYEES" 'cornice'

зама́зка "zah MAH skuh" 'putty'

ре́зка "RYE skuh" 'cutting'

виртуо́з "vyir too AWS" 'virtuoso'

З represents an "s" sound under the same conditions that make в stand for an "f" rather than a "v" (sections 4.2 and 4.3): before a voiceless consonant (as in сказка) and at the end of a word.

Э: "Y-less E"

13.1

19

э = e	Э = E

Э́мма "EM muh" 'Emma'

э́ра "E ruh" 'era'

э́хо "E khuh" 'echo'

э́тика "EI tyi kuh" 'ethics'

маэ́стро "mah E struh" 'maestro'

This letter is called *e oborótnoye* ("E ah bah RAWT-nuh yuh"), which means the 'turned-around *e*'. It is used to write a plain *e* ("e" or "ei")—that is, an *e* that has no "y" or soft consonant before it. That is much rarer than you would expect. In native Russian words it is practically limited to the word for 'this' (э́тот "E tuht") and a few closely related words. Otherwise, when you see э in a word, you can be almost sure that the word was borrowed from some other language.

Here are a few examples with the э in an unaccented syllable; it is most frequent, as these examples show, at the beginning of a word. The sound is a somewhat relaxed "e":

эми́р "e MYEER" 'emir'

этике́т "e tyi KYET" 'etiquette'

эконо́мика "e kah NAW myi kuh" 'economics'

эскимо́с "e skyee MAWS" 'Eskimo'

эсто́нский "e STAWN ski" 'Estonian'

аэрона́вт "ah e rah NAHFT" 'aeronaut'

экстра́кт "e KSTRAHKT" 'extract'

эско́рт "e SKAWRT" 'escort'

экиво́ки "e kyi VAW kyee" 'quibble'

13.2

You will not very often see э after a consonant. It occurs in some representations of foreign words, such as мэр "MER" for English *mayor*, and сэр "SER" for *sir*, and Тэн "TEN" for the French *Taine*. It is also used in writing the names of the letters: вэ ve "VE", тэ "TE", and others. Э appears in the original of *nep*, which is an acronym from *nóvaya ekonomícheskaya polítika* 'the New Economic Policy'; э is the first letter in *ekonomícheskaya* and the middle letter in *nep* (нэп). Compare экономика in section 13.1.

13.3

экза́мен "e GZAH myin" 'examination'

эски́з "e SKYEES" 'sketch' (French *esquisse*)

энтузиа́ст "en too zyi AHST" 'enthusiast'

энтузиа́зм "en too zyi AHZM" 'enthusiasm'

экста́з "e KSTAHS" 'ecstasy'

Your eye has to get used to distinguishing the vowel letter э from the consonant letter з. Students often have some trouble with this. The words above are some in which both letters occur; they help to point up both the similarity and the difference.

Экза́мен "e GZAH myin" in the preceding section also contains the first example of assimilation of a voiceless consonant to one that is voiced: what is written *kz* is pronounced "gz". The direction of the change is the same as in previous examples of assimilation: the first consonant is affected by the one that follows. The second being voiced, the voiceless one before it is replaced by the corresponding voiced sound: where *k* is written, the sound is a "g"; a *t* would change to a "d", an *s* to a "z", and so on.

This change does not take place before all voiced consonants. It occurs before a *b* (б), *d* (д), *g* (г), *z* (з), or *zh* (ж), not before an *l* (л), *m* (м), *n* (н), *r* (р), or *v* (в).

Г ("GE"): G

14.1

г = g	Г = G

газ "GAHS" 'gas'

газе́та "gah ZYE tuh" 'newspaper'

Гага́рин "gah GAH ryin" 'Gagarin'

Григо́рий "gryee GAW ryee" 'Grigori, Gregory'

рагу́ "rah GOO" 'ragout'

тайга́ "tai GAH" 'taiga'

The next letters you will meet are five that are more or less straight out of the Greek alphabet. This one is gamma (Γ), and stands for the "g" sound as in *go*. Its name in Russian is гэ "GE".

Here are some more examples:

грани́т "grah NYEET" 'granite'

грима́са "gryee MAH suh" 'grimace'

ага́т "ah GAHT" 'agate'

анга́р "ahn GAHR" 'hangar'

а́вгуст "AH vgoost" 'August'

ваго́н "vah GAWN" 'car' (French *wagon*)

Ниага́ра "nyi ah GAH ruh" 'Niagara'

Огонёк "ah gah NYAWK" 'Ogonëk' 'Ogonyok'

о́рган "AWR guhn" 'organ (of the body)'

14.2

гитáра "gyee TAH ruh" 'guitar'

гéний "GYEI nyee" 'genius'

Геóргий "gyi AWR gyee" 'Georgi (George)'

Тургéнев "toor GYEI nyif" 'Turgenev'

Кирги́з "kyeer GYEES" 'Kirghiz'

A "soft g" in Russian is a "g" pronounced with the tongue aiming for the "y" position (section 7.3). In the pronunciations we indicate this by writing "gy". The Russian г never represents what we call a "soft g", which is a "j" sound, as in *George*.

More examples with the Russian "soft g":

ген "GYEN" 'gene'

Гéрман "GYER muhn" 'German'

гигáнт "gyee GAHNT" 'giant'

Евгéний "yi VGYEI nyee" 'Yevgeni (Eugene)'

Онéгин "ah NYEI gyin" 'Onegin'

Сергéй "syir GYEI" 'Sergei'

Сергéев "syir GYEI yif" 'Sergeyev'

14.3

гонг "GAWN|K" 'gong'

ми́тинг "MYEE tyin|k" 'meeting'

грог "GRAWK" 'grog'

зигзáг "zyee GZAHK" 'zigzag'

At the end of a word "g" is replaced by the corresponding voiceless sound, which is "k". A good example is рог "RAWK", which means 'horn'. The place name Кривой Рог "kryee VOI RAWK" means 'crooked horn.'

14.4

Before a voiceless consonant, "g" is sometimes replaced by "k", as in:

Му́соргский "MOO suhrk ski" 'Musorgsky, Moussorgsky'

Before к or т, however, г represents the "kh" sound. Examples of this are in the common words но́гти "NAW-khtyee" 'nails' and ко́гти "KAW khtyee" 'claws'.

14.5

гаре́м "gah RYEM" 'harem'

геро́й "gyi ROI" 'hero'

ге́тман "GYET muhn" 'hetman'

гуса́р "goo SAHR" 'hussar'

Гайава́та "guh yah VAH tuh" 'Hiawatha'

могика́не "muh gyee KAH nyi" 'Mohicans'

One of the oddest things about the behavior of г, from our point of view at least, is that it sometimes represents an *h* in words borrowed from other languages. The reason for this is purely historical. It is a convention that started in Kiev, because in Ukrainian (and in Church Slavic) г represents a sound that is roughly like our "h".

More examples of this:

Гава́на "gah VAH nuh" 'Havana'

Гаи́ти "gah EE tyee" 'Haiti'

гама́к "gah MAHK" 'hammock'

гие́на "gyee YE nuh" 'hyena'

гигие́на "gyee gyee YE nuh" 'hygiene'

Гоме́р "gah MYER" 'Homer'

гормо́н "gahr MAWN" 'hormone'

грамм "GRAHM" 'gram'

грамма́тика "grah MAH tyi kuh" 'grammar'

контраге́нт "kuhn trah GYENT" 'contractor'

круг "KROOK" 'circle'

круго́вой "kroo gah VOI" 'circular'

геро́йский "gyi ROI ski" 'heroic'

интри́га "een TRYEE guh" 'intrigue'

аргуме́нт "ahr goo MYENT" 'argument'

магни́т "mah GNYEET" 'magnet'

са́га "SAH guh" 'saga'

сегме́нт "syi GMYENT" 'segment'

гангре́на "gahn GRYE nuh" 'gangrene'

аге́нт "ah GYENT" 'agent'

аге́нтство "ah GYEN tstvuh" 'agency'

миг "MYEEK" 'instant'

ми́гом "MYEE guhm" 'in a flash'

острога́ "ah strah GAH" 'gaff' 'harpoon'

горизо́нт "guh ryi ZAWNT" 'horizon'

гармо́ника "guhr MAW nyi kuh" 'accordion'

Д ("DE"): D

15.1

д = d	Д = D

да "DAH" 'yes'

да́ма "DAH muh" 'lady'

Достое́вский "duh stah YEF ski" 'Dostoyevsky'

о́да "AW duh" 'ode'

Годуно́в "guh doo NAWF" 'Godunov'

ту́ндра "TOON druh" 'tundra'

This letter has a somewhat more elaborate design than its prototype, but quite clearly was patterned upon the Greek delta (Δ). It is the Russian equivalent of *d*, and is called дэ "DE".

The Russian "d" sound, like the "t" and the "n", is a dental, made with the tip of the tongue touching the back of the upper teeth.

Here are more examples for you to practice with:

до́за "DAW zuh" 'dose'

дом "DAWM" 'house'

Дон "DAWN" 'the Don (River)'

дра́ма "DRAH muh" 'drama'

Андре́й "ahn DRYEI" 'Andrei (Andrew)'

Андре́ев "ahn DRYEI yif" 'Andreyev'

Ноздрёв "nah ZDRYAWF" 'Nozdrëv, Nozdryoff'

со́да "SAW duh" 'soda'

дро́тик "DRAW tyik" 'dart' 'javelin'

данти́ст "dahn TYEEST" 'dentist'

друг "DROOK" 'friend'.

15.2

де́мон "DYEH muhn" 'demon'

студе́нт "stoo DYENT" 'student'

диск "DYEESK" 'disk' 'discus'

идио́т "ee dyi AWT" 'idiot'

ра́дио "RAH dyi aw" 'radio'

For a soft "d", in де and ди in these examples, the tip of the tongue is held down (section 7.3), so that when you undertake to make a "d" sound a stretch of the tongue back from the tip makes contact with the gum ridge and a little of the hard palate. The "dy" in the simulated pronunciations is the best we can do to suggest the result by comparison to English sounds.

More examples with soft "d":

демаго́г "dyi mah GAWK" 'demagogue'

диагра́мма "dyi ah GRAHM muh" 'diagram'

дина́мо "dyee NAH muh" 'dynamo'

кандида́т "kuhn dyee DAHT" 'candidate'

ра́дий "RAH dyee" 'radium'

сарди́на "sahr DYEE nuh" 'sardine'

стадио́н "stuh dyi AWN" 'stadium'

ме́дик "MYEI dyik" 'medical student'

медикаме́нт "myi dyi kah MYENT" 'medicine'

15.3

во́дка "VAWT kuh" 'vodka'

This old acquaintance points up the difference between Russian speech habits and ours in pronouncing abutting consonants like the *-dk-* written here. There is nothing that keeps us from saying "VAHD kuh", as the English spelling suggests; but before a voiceless consonant the "d" in Russian is replaced by a "t"; hence: "VAWT kuh".

The following words show the same replacement of *d* by *t* because of a following *k*:

га́дкий "GAHT ki" 'nasty'

загоро́дка "zuh gah RAWT kuh" 'fence'

и́зредка "EE zryit kuh" 'now and then'

15.4

ме́тод "MYE tuht" 'method'

маскара́д "muh skah RAHT" 'masquerade'

комо́д "kah MAWT" 'commode'

"D" is also replaced by "t' at the end of a word. Here are a few more examples of that:

Самое́д "suh mah YET" 'Samoyede'

Но́вгород "NAW vguh ruht" 'Novgorod'

го́род "GAW ruht" 'town' 'city'

град "GRAHT" 'hail'

норд "NAWRT" 'north'

Л: L

16.1

л = l	Л = L

ла́ва "LAH vuh" 'lava'

Ломоно́сов "luh mah NAW suhf" 'Lomonosov'

кула́к "koo LAHK" 'kulak'

Во́лга "VAWL guh" 'Volga'

Волгогра́д "vuhl gah GRAHT" 'Volgograd'

Толсто́й "tahl STOI" 'Tolstoy'

Ура́л "oo RAHL" 'Urals'

Владивосто́к "vluh dyi vah STAWK" 'Vladivostok'

There is a complication that keeps me from quoting the Russian name of this letter. Л corresponds to our *l*, and the name is similar to "el", which will do for the time being.

The form is derived, with slight modifications, from the Greek lambda (Λ).

More examples for reading practice:

Ла́ра "LAH ruh" 'Lara'

луна́ "loo NAH" 'moon'

Влади́мир "vlah DYEE myir" 'Vladimir'

Глазуно́в "gluh zoo NAWF" 'Glazunov'

Станисла́вский "stuh nyee SLAHF ski" 'Stanislavsky'

колхо́з "kahl KHAWS" 'kolkhoz'

кана́л "kah NAHL" 'canal'

Крокоди́л "kruh kah DYEEL" '(the magazine) Krokodil'

Михаи́л "myee khah EEL" 'Mikhail (Michael)'

вокза́л "vah GZAHL" 'railway station' (from Vauxhall)

и́дол "EE duhl" 'idol'

идеа́л "ee dyi AHL" 'ideal'

а́нгел "AHN gyil" 'angel'

ко́нсул "KAWN sool" 'consul'

катало́г "kuh tah LAWK" 'catalog'

16.2

ли́га "LYEE guh" 'league'

литерату́ра "lyee tyi rah TOO ruh" 'literature'

Лев "LYEF" 'Lev (Leo)'

Еле́на "yi LYE nuh" 'Yelena (Helen)'

диале́кт "dyi ah LYEKT" 'dialect'

хулига́н "khoo lyee GAHN" 'hooligan'

The soft "l", made with the tongue bunched in the front of the mouth (section 7.3), is much like the palatal "l" sounds of Spanish (Castilian *ll*), Portuguese (*lh*), and Italian (*gl*). Like those sounds, it has no close parallel in English; we have to represent it as "ly".

Further examples with soft "l":

Ле́нин "LYEI nyin" 'Lenin'

Ленингра́д "lyi nyin GRAHT" 'Leningrad'

Ле́рмонтов "LYER muhn tuhf" 'Lermontov'

ли́дер "LYEE dyir" 'leader'

лимо́н "lyee MAWN" 'lemon'

лимона́д "lyee mah NAHT" 'lemonade'

Васи́лий "vah SYEE lyee" 'Vasili (Basil)'

Гли́нка "GLYEEN kuh" 'Glinka'

диле́мма "dyee LYEM muh" 'dilemma'

Менде́леев "myin dyi LYEI yif" 'Mendeleyev'

Ста́лин "STAH lyin" 'Stalin'

ана́лиз "ah NAH lyis" 'analysis'

атле́т "ah TLYET" 'athlete'

делега́т "dyi lyi GAHT" 'delegate'

колле́га "kah LYE guh" 'colleague'

миллиме́тр "myi lyi MYETR" 'millimeter'

телегра́мма "tyi lyi GRAHM muh" 'telegram'

элева́тор "e lyi VAH tuhr" 'elevator'

П ("PE"): P

17.1

п = p	П = P

пáпа "PAH puh" 'papa'

Пáвлов "PAH vluhf" 'Pavlov'

Прáвда "PRAH vduh" 'Pravda'

прáвда "PRAH vduh" 'truth'

спýтник "SPOOT nyik" 'satellite' 'sputnik'

суп "SOOP" 'soup'

Almost everyone gets exposed to pi as a Greek small letter (π) used as a mathematical symbol. The Greek capital is a simpler structure of the same general shape (Π). It was the model for this Russian equivalent of our *p*. Its Russian name is пэ "PE".

Like "t" and "k" (section 2.2), the Russian "p" is pronounced without aspiration.

More examples for reading practice:

Еврóпа "yi VRAW puh" 'Europe'

Панáма "pah NAH muh" 'Panama'

пáрка "PAHR kuh" 'parka'

план "PLAHN" 'plan'

планéта "plah NYE tuh" 'planet'

подзóл "pah DZAWL" 'podzol'

Попо́в "pah PAWF" 'Popov'

пропага́нда "pruh pah GAHN duh" 'propaganda'

пу́динг "POO dyin|k" 'pudding'

диплома́т "dyi plah MAHT" 'diplomat'

прое́кт "pruh YEKT" 'project (noun)'

спорт "SPAWRT" 'sport'

эпо́ха "eh PAW khuh" 'epoch'

аппара́т "ah pah RAHT" 'apparatus'

грип "GRYEEP" 'influenza' 'grippe'

17.2

пило́т "pyee LAWT" 'pilot'

Пётр "PYAWTR" 'Pëtr, Pyotr (Peter)'

Петро́в "pyi TRAWF" 'Petrov'

капита́н "kuh pyee TAHN" 'captain'

копе́йка "kah PYEI kuh" 'kopeck'

Before a е or an и, п represents a soft "p", made with the tongue raised and bunched in the front of the mouth (section 7.3). The suggestion of "py" exaggerates the effect, but once again is the best we can do to make note of the contrast with the ordinary (hard) "p".

Further examples with soft "p":

аппети́т "ah pyi TYEET" 'appetite'

о́пера "AW pyi ruh"

пери́од "pyi RYEE uht" 'period'

Пе́ру "PYE roo" 'Peru'

пикни́к "pyeek NYEEK" 'picnic'

пионе́р "pyi ah NYEER" 'pioneer'

температу́ра "tyim pyi rah TOO ruh" 'temperature'

капитали́ст "kuh pyi tah LYEEST" 'capitalist'

Ф ("EF"): F

18.1

ф = f	Ф = F

факт "FAHKT" 'fact'

Фрол "FRAWL" 'Frol'

фоно́граф "fah NAW gruhf" 'phonograph'

А́фрика "AH fryi kuh" 'Africa'

софа́ "sah FAH" 'sofa'

сифо́н "syee FAWN" 'siphon'

Ио́сиф "i AW syif" 'Joseph'

Аэрофло́т "ah e rah FLAWT" 'Aeroflot (Russian airline)'

This is эф "EF", which is equivalent to our *f*. The letter is from the Greek phi (Φ), and it often corresponds to our digraph *ph* in words or word parts (such as *phono*- and -*graph*) of Greek origin.

More examples:

авто́граф "ah FTAW gruhf" 'autograph'

кафта́н "kah FTAHN" 'caftan'

лифт "LYEEFT" 'lift'

ни́мфа "NYEEM fuh" 'nymph'

сарафа́н "suh rah FAHN" 'sarafan'

тари́ф "tah RYEEF" 'tariff'

трию́мф "tryi OOMF" 'triumph'

Уфа́ "oo FAH" 'Ufa'

фарс "FAHRS" 'farce'

фаса́д "fah SAHT" 'facade'

флаг "FLAHK" 'flag'

фо́сфор "FAW sfuhr" 'phosphorus'

фронт "FRAWNT" 'front'

телефо́н "tyi lyi FAWN" 'telephone'

платфо́рма "plaht FAWR muh" 'platform'

эффе́кт "e FYEKT" 'effect'

18.2

фи́га "FYEE guh" 'fig'

Фигаро́ "fyee gah RAW" 'Figaro'

фи́рма "FYEER muh" 'firm'

фе́рма "FYER muh" 'farm'

сфе́ра "SFYE ruh" 'sphere'

ко́фе "KAW fyi" 'coffee'

"Fy" in the simulated pronunciations stands for the soft "f" (section 7.3), rather than a sequence of "f" and "y" sounds. The soft "f" is indicated by the spellings фе and фи in the examples above. Here are a few more:

конфе́та "kahn FYE tuh" 'candy'

конфетти́ "kahn fyi TYEE" 'confetti'

профе́ссор "prah FYE suhr" 'professor'

сапфи́р "sah PFYEER" 'sapphire'

фиа́ско "fyi AH skuh" 'fiasco'

фигу́ра "fyee GOO ruh" 'figure'

фи́зика "FYEE zyi kuh" 'physics'

филóсоф "fyee LAW suhf" 'philosopher'

фемини́стка "fyi myi NYEEST kuh" 'feminist'

трофéй "trah FYEI" 'trophy'

18.3

Фёдор "FYAW duhr" 'Fëdor, Fyodor (Theodore)'

Фомá "fah MAH" 'Foma (Thomas)'

Мáрфа "MAHR fuh" 'Martha'

миф "MYEEF" 'myth'

арифмéтика "ah ryee FMYEI tyi kuh" 'arithmetic'

The sound that we spell with *th* in many words of Greek origin corresponds to a similar Greek sound that is spelled with the letter theta (θ). But there is no "th" sound in Russian. In Russian words or word elements derived from Greek, theta is usually replaced by an "f" sound, spelled with this letter ф. Here are a few more examples:

пáфос "PAH fuhs" 'pathos'

логари́фм "luh gah RYEEFM" 'logarithm'

Афанáсий "ah fah NAH syee" 'Afanasi, Athanasius'

Голиáф "guh lyi AHF" 'Goliath'

Пифагóр "pyee fah GAWR" 'Pythagoras'

кáфедра "KAH fyi druh" 'rostrum' 'pulpit'

анáфема "ah NAH fyi muh" 'anathema'

However, many words in which we have *th* representing the Greek theta reached Russian through languages such as Latin, German, French, and Polish, in which there is no "th" sound. In such cases, Russian has a *t* corresponding to our *th*. Some examples of that are:

термóметр "tyir MAW myitr" 'thermometer'

теорéма "tyi ah RYE muh" 'theorem'

трон "TRAWN" 'throne'

Russian conventionally replaces our *th* with т. Our word *method* may be the source of Russian ме́тод "MYE-tuht". And т replaces our *th* in transliterated names such as:

Смит "SMYEET 'Smith'

Торо́ "taw RAW" 'Thoreau'

Са́утпорт "SAH oot pawrt" 'Southport'

Форт-Уэ́рт "fawrt oo ERT" 'Fort Worth'

A curious pair are ритм "RYEETM" 'rhythm' and ри́фма "RYEE fmuh" 'rhyme'; the first, showing by its form that it came through French (*rythme*), keeps the sense of Greek *rhythmós*; the second has -ф- representing the *-th-* of the Greek word, but has an alteration of form (the ending -a) and a shift of meaning.

Б ("BE"): B

19.1

б = b	Б = B

брат "BRAHT" 'brother'

бóмба "BAWM buh" 'bomb'

балалáйка "buh lah LAI kuh" 'balalaika'

Бакý "bah KOO" 'Baku'

Бородúн "buh rah DYEEN" 'Borodin'

табáк "tah BAHK" 'tobacco'

акробáт "ah krah BAHT" 'acrobat'

банк "BAN|K" 'bank'

All of the remaining letters have shapes that do not coincide either with our Latin letters or with Greek letters.

This is the only one for which you will have to learn different shapes for the capital and for the small letter. It corresponds to our *b* and is called бэ "BE".

A new *b* had to be created for the Slavic alphabet because, as you have seen, the Greek beta was preempted to spell the Slavic "v" sound.

Here are some further examples for reading practice:

Байкáл "bai KAHL" 'Baikal'

бамбýк "bahm BOOK" 'bamboo'

блонди́нка "blahn DYEEN kuh" 'blonde'

Бухара́ "boo khah RAH" 'Bukhara'

изба́ "ee ZBAH" 'izba'

комба́йн "kahm BAIN" 'combine (noun)'

Обло́мов "ah BLAW muhf" 'Oblomov'

пробле́ма "prah BLYE muh" 'problem'

тромбо́н "trahm BAWN" 'trombone'

Хаба́ровск "khah BAH ruhfsk" 'Khabarovsk'

колбаса́ "kuhl bah SAH" 'saussage'

буй "BOO i" 'buoy'

19.2

In бе and би, б stands for a soft "b" (section 7.3), which we indicate by writing "by" in the approximated pronunciations. Here are some examples:

белу́га "byi LOO guh" 'beluga'

Безу́хов "byi ZOO khuhf" 'Bezukhov'

белору́с "byi lah ROOS" 'Bielorussian'

бива́к "byee VAHK" 'bivouac'

бизо́н "byee ZAWN" 'bison'

боби́на "bah BYEE nuh" 'bobbin'

Тибе́т "tyee BYET" 'Tibet'

турби́на "toor BYEE nuh" 'turbine'

узбе́к "oo ZBYEK" 'Uzbek'

орби́та "ahr BYEE tuh" 'orbit'

19.3

клуб "KLOOP" 'club'

микро́б "myee KRAWP" 'microbe'

Боб Хоп "BAWP KHAWP" 'Bob Hope'

краб "KRAHP" 'crab'

At the end of a word, "b" is replaced by the corresponding voiceless consonant, which is "p".

The same unvoicing occurs when б comes before a voiceless consonant, as in:

Ви́тебск "VYEE tyipsk" 'Vitebsk'

абсу́рд "ah PSOORT" 'absurdity'

субстра́т "soo PSTRAHT" 'substratum'

субтро́пики "soop TRAW pyi kyee" 'subtropics'

19.4

футбо́л "food BAWL" 'football'

асбе́ст "ah ZBYEST" 'asbestos'

When б is the second consonant in a pair, the consonant before it is voiced, even when the letter is one that otherwise represents a voiceless consonant. That is why the т in футбол is pronounced "d", and the с in асбест is pronounced "z".

The assimilation is like that which turns the к in экзамен into a "g" (section 13.4).

LESSON TWENTY

Я ("YAH"): YA

20.1

я = ya	Я = Ya

Я́лта "YAHL tuh" 'Yalta'

я́хта "YAH khtuh" 'yacht'

боя́ре "bah YAH ryi" 'boyars'

Росси́я "rah SYEE yuh" 'Russia'

This letter is called *ya* ("YAH"). At the beginning of a word or after a vowel, when accented, it stands for sounds ("yah") like the *ya* in *yacht*. At the end of a word, unaccented, it represents "ya" with the same reduced or "neutral" vowel that is spelled with a in words such as тройка and Правда.

A few more examples of the same kind:

Я́ва "YAH vuh" 'Java'

а́рия "AH ryi yuh" 'aria'

би́блия "BYEE blyi yuh" 'bible'

иде́я "ee DYEI yuh" 'idea'

Изве́стия "ee ZVYEI styi yuh" 'Izvestia'

гармо́ния "gahr MAW nyi yuh" 'harmony'

па́ртия "PAHR tyi yuh" 'party'

поэ́зия "pah EI zyi yuh" 'poetry'

фая́нс "fah YAHNS" 'faience'

20.2

Ля́дов "LYAH duhf" 'Liadov'

Дя́гилев "DYAH gyi lyif" 'Diaghileff'

Со́ня "SAW nyuh" 'Sonya, Sonia'

Та́ня "TAH nyuh" 'Tanya, Tania'

Examples such as these show you the real utility of this letter. The value of я after a consonant can still be said to be "ya" if it is understood that the "y" is combined in the preceding soft consonant, like the "y" of "ye" (section 7.3). The "lya" and "dya" and "nya" of these examples mean soft "l" plus "a", soft "d" plus "a", and soft "n" plus "a", respectively. The letter я is one of the indicators of the soft consonants, one of the means by which Russian avoids having separate letters for the hard and soft consonants.

Some further examples:

Бердя́ев "byir DYAH yif" 'Berdyayev'

Ва́ня "VAH nyuh" 'Vanya'

Вя́тка "VYAHT kuh" 'Vyatka'

Но́вая Земля́ "NAW vuh yuh zyim LYAH" 'Novaya Zemlya'

Пе́тя "PYEI tyuh" 'Petya'

Скря́бин "SKRYAH byin" 'Scriabin'

Я́сная Поля́на "YAH snuh yuh pah LYAH nuh" 'Yasnaya Polyana'

20.3

ля́псус "LYAH psoos" 'lapsus'

Аля́ска "ah LYAH skuh" 'Alaska'

Золя́ "zaw LYAH" 'Zola'

The frequent occurrence of soft "l" in these and similar words needs a special note of explanation. The

Russian hard "l" even before a vowel is a very hollow sound much like our "l" in *ball* and *wool*. The "l" of some other languages, especially French and German, is apt to strike the Russians as more like their soft "l", and this is reflected in borrowed words and transliterations.

20.4

Яку́тск "yi KOOTSK" 'Yakutsk'

Япо́ния "yi PAW nyi yuh" 'Japan'

Маяко́вский "muh yi KAWF ski" 'Mayakovsky'

Пятиго́рск "pyi tyee GAWRSK" 'Pyatigorsk'

пятиле́тка "pyi tyee LYET kuh" 'pyatiletka (five-year plan)'

Хомяко́в "khuh myi KAWF" 'Khomyakov'

In an unaccented syllable at the beginning of or inside a word, я stands for the same sound or sounds as though е were written: "yi" or "i" after a soft consonant, in which the vowel is rather like our "short i" or a relaxed "ee" (section 7.4). But "yah" or "yeh" may be heard for я when these words are spoken with intentional slowness, especially when one is pronounced alone.

Ю ("YOO"): YU

21.1

ю = yu	Ю = Yu

ю́мор "YOO muhr" 'humor'

ю́рта "YOOR tuh" 'yurt'

Ю́рий "YOO ryee" 'Yuri (George)'

Ю́лия "YOO lyi yuh" 'Julia'

юбиле́й "yoo byee LYEI" 'jubilee'

Юпи́тер "yoo PYEE tyir" 'Jupiter'

Сове́тский Сою́з "sah VYET ski sah YOOS" 'the Soviet Union'

Югосла́вия "yoo gah SLAH vyi yuh" 'Yugoslavia'

ювели́р "yoo vyi LYEER" 'jeweler'

юг "YOOK" 'south'

This letter's name is *yu*, which of course sounds like the name of our letter *u* ("YOO"). At the beginning of a word or after a vowel it represents "yoo" (like the *yu* in *Yule*).

бюрокра́т "byoo rah KRAHT" 'bureaucrat'

валю́та "vah LYOO tuh" 'valuta'

Милюко́в "myee lyoo KAWF" 'Milyukov'

нюа́нс "nyoo AHNS" 'nuance'

салю́т "sah LYOOT" 'salute'

When ю follows a consonant, it indicates a soft consonant plus "oo", just as е indicates a soft consonant plus "eh" (section 7.3), ё a soft consonant plus "aw" (section 8.1), и a soft consonant plus "ee" (section 9.2), and я a soft consonant plus "ah" (section 20.2).

Very often in borrowed words or transliterated names, ю represents French *u* or German *ü*.

Some further examples:

брюне́тка "bryoo NYET kuh" 'brunette'

Добролю́бов "duh brah LYOO buhf" 'Dobrolyubov'

костю́м "kah STYOOM" 'costume'

Кюи́ "kyoo EE" 'Cui'

кюри́ "kyoo RYEE" 'curie'

сюрпри́з "syoor PRYEES" 'surprise'

тюк "TYOOK" 'package'

лю́стра "LYOO struh" 'luster'

лютера́нский "lyoo tyi RAHN ski" 'Lutheran'

ы ("yi REE"): Y ("ee" after a hard consonant)

22.1

ы = y

Кулы́гин "koo LEE gyin" 'Kulygin'

Крым "KREEM" 'Crimea'

му́зыка "MOO zi kuh" 'music'

Крыло́в "kri LAWF" 'Krylov'

Салтыко́в "suhl ti KAWF" 'Saltykov'

ярлы́к "yir LEEK" 'label'

Up to this point you have seen five vowels, the way of writing all five of them after soft consonants, and the way of writing four of them after hard consonants. For a summary, we can tabulate these details like this:

	"ah"	"e"	"ee"	"aw"	"oo"
after a hard consonant:	а	э	□	о	у
after a soft consonant:	я	е	и	ё	ю

The letter that is needed to fill the box in this table is ы. In unaccented syllables the sound it represents is much like what we spell with a *y* in *rhythm*, that is, our "short i" sound. Thus when speakers of English transliterate ы, *y* is usually employed so as to distinguish it from *i* for и. In accented syllables the sound is too tense to be compared with our "short i" sound; our closest substitute for it is "ee". The essential difference in a pair such as Нил "NYEEL" 'the Nile' and ныл "NEEL" 'whined' is that the first has a soft and the latter a hard "n".

But that is not the whole story. No matter what decisions we have to make in comparing these sounds to English sounds, there is an appreciable difference between the vowels in Нил "NYEEL" and ныл "NEEL". For Russian и and for our "ee" the tongue is raised high in the front of the mouth. This is similar to the tongue position for a soft consonant (section 7.3); it is no wonder that the и following a soft consonant has a good sharp sound that we easily identify with our *ee*. But when the preceding consonant is hard, the tongue *avoids* the bunching in the front of the mouth that characterizes the soft consonants. The vowel ы ("ee" after a hard consonant) is made with the *middle* of the tongue raised toward the roof of the mouth. The tongue elevation moves back from the usual front position for "ee" toward, but not to, the back position that goes with an "oo" sound. The result is a somewhat duller sound than what we think of as the "ee" in *kneel*; but the vowel in *nil* lacks the necessary tenseness of the Russian ы when it is stressed.

The Russians sometimes call this letter simply ы, that is, by making the sound that it represents. An older and much handier name, especially for our purposes, is еры́ "yi REE".

Here are a few more examples that contain this letter:

Рыле́ев "ri LYEI yif" 'Ryleyev'

Колыма́ "kuh li MAH" 'Kolyma'

Лоды́гин "lah DEE gyin" 'Lodygin'

язы́к "yi ZEEK" 'language'

языкозна́ние "yi zi kah ZNAH nyi yuh" 'linguistics'

22.2

Very often this ы at the end of a word is the indicator of a noun in the plural. It has that function in these examples:

тата́ры "tah TAH ri" 'Tatars' 'Tartars'

мокаси́ны "muh kah SYEE ni" 'moccasins'

А́нды "AHN di" 'Andes'

Карпа́ты "kahr PAH ti" 'Carpathians'

гу́ны "GOO ni" 'Huns'

самое́ды "suh mah YE di" 'Samoyedes'

эскимо́сы "e skyee MAW si" 'Eskimos'

фина́нсы "fyee NAHN si" 'finances'

Афи́ны "ah FYEE ni" 'Athens' (Greek *Athenai*)

22.3

кумы́с "koo MWEES" 'kumiss'

Громы́ко "grah MWEE kuh" 'Gromyko'

Румы́ния "roo MWEE nyi yuh" 'Romania'

Вы́борг "VWEE buhrk" 'Vyborg'

не́рвы "NYER vwi" 'nerves'

Бы́ков "BWEE kuhf" 'Bykov'

были́на "bwi LYEE nuh" 'legend'

пылесо́с "pwi lyi SAWS" 'dust-sucker, i.e., vacuum cleaner'

фы́ркал "FWEER kuhl" 'snorted (of a horse)'

The "w" in the simulated pronunciations of these examples is an exaggeration, but here again it is probably better to exaggerate than to ignore. There is a fleeting suggestion of a "w" in the transition from one of the consonants that involve lip action ("m, v, b, p, f") to this vowel. This is not the only situation in which there is some tendency toward a "w" effect in Russian hard consonants, but this one is particularly worth noting because plain "mee, vee, bee, pee, fee" or "mi, vi, bi, pi, fi" lacks any suggestion of the peculiar acoustic effect of one of these consonants (м, к, б, п, ф) followed by ы.

Following is more practice:

вы "VWEE" 'you'

мы "MWEE" 'we'

пыл "PWEEL" 'ardor' 'passion'

пы́лкий "PWEEL ki" 'passionate'

бык "BWEEK" 'ox'

22.4

Бе́лый "BYE li" 'Biely'

бе́лый "BYE li" 'white'

Будённый "boo DYAWN ni" 'Budenny'

Кра́сный Крест "KRAH sni KRYEST" 'Red Cross'

Но́вый Мир "NAW vwi MYEER" 'Novy Mir' ("The New World")

Like any other vowel, ы can be combined with й to form a diphthong. This diphthong ый occurs mainly as an ending of adjectives and of names that are adjectives in form, like the examples above. The acoustic effect is roughly like that of what we write with *-i* in *chili* and with *-y* in *chilly*. I have used "i" in the approximated pronunciations partly because that seems less than "y" would be, and partly because *y* is already overworked.

Here are some additional examples:

ста́рый "STAH ri" 'old'

краси́вый "krah SYEE vwi" 'beautiful'

за́падный "ZAH puhd ni" 'western'

ве́рный "VYER ni" 'true'

Ива́н Гро́зный "ee VAHN GRAW zni" 'Ivan the Terrible'

Ш ("SHAH"): SH

23.1

ш = sh	Ш = Sh

шко́ла "SHKAW luh" 'school'

Шо́лохов "SHAW luh khuhf" 'Sholokhov'

Ната́ша "nah TAH shuh" 'Natasha'

Ирты́ш "eer TEESH" 'Irtysh'

шлюз "SHLYOOS" 'sluice'

Sha ("SHAH") represents a sound we also have in English but which we spell with a digraph: *sh*. Greek provided no letter for this sound, and one had to be devised for writing Old Slavic. The suggestion for the form very likely came from a three-pronged letter that you may have seen in the Hebrew original of *kosher*.

Here are some more examples for reading drill:

шта́ты "SHTAH ṭi" 'states'

штурм "SHTOORM" 'storming (military)'

шторм "SHTAWRM" 'storm (weather)'

штаны́ "shtah NEE" 'trousers'

шпио́н "shpyee AWN" 'spy'

Шу́йский "SHOOY ski" 'Shuisky'

Са́ша "SAH shuh" 'Sasha'

Алёша "ah LYAW shuh" 'Alësha, Alyosha'

душ "DOOSH" 'shower' (French *douche*)

марш "MAHRSH" 'march'

ма́ршал "MAHR shuhl" 'marshal'

Пу́шкин "POO shkyin" 'Pushkin'

Петру́шка "pyi TROO shkuh" 'Petrushka, Petrouchka'

куку́шка "koo KOO shkuh" 'cuckoo'

Then there is ба́бушка "BAH boo shkuh" 'grandmother', which we lifted in English to name a kind of headdress—but we pronounce the word "buh BOOSH kuh".

23.2

шеф "SHEF" 'chief'

шёлк "SHAWLK" 'silk'

маши́на "mah SHEE nuh" 'machine'

гало́ши "gah LAW shi" 'galoshes'

шифр "SHEEFR" 'cipher'

The "sh" sound represented by *sha* is always hard. You never have to try to mix a "y" sound with it as you do for a soft consonant. That is why no "y" is written in the approximated pronunciations of these examples. ше is simply "SHE" and шё is simply "SHAW". And since ш represents a hard consonant, the и in ши stands for the dull, rather muffled "ee" sound that was discussed in section 22.1; that is, ши is pronounced as if it were written шы.

Here are some more examples of ше and ши:

шейх "SHEIKH" 'sheikh'

шери́ф "shi RYEEF" 'sheriff'

Ку́йбышев "KOOY bwi shif" 'Kuibyshev'

Выши́нский "vwi SHEEN ski" 'Vyshinsky'

Ши́шкин "SHEE shkyin" 'Shishkin'

Шишко́в "shi SHKAWF" 'Shishkov'

Га́ршин "GAHR shin" 'Garshin'

23.3

A ю (yu) would not ordinarily be written after a hard consonant. Because ю is the conventional representation of French *u* and German *ü* in words borrowed from those languages, we do find шю written in words such as

парашю́т "puh rah SHOOT" 'parachute'

брошюра "brah SHOO ruh" 'brochure'

in which the ю has no effect on the hardness of the ш before it; шю is pronounced exactly as though шу were written, that is, "SHOO".

23.4

Шаля́пин "shah LYAH pyin" or "shi LYAH pyin" 'Chaliapin'

шашлы́к "shah SHLEEK" or "shi SHLEEK" 'shashlik'

шама́н "shah MAHN" 'shaman'

шампа́нское "shahm PAHN skuh yuh" 'champagne'

шара́да "shah RAH duh" 'charade'

шасси́ "shahs SYEE" 'chassis'

шофёр "shah FYAWR" 'chauffeur'

шокола́д "shuh kah LAHT" 'chocolate'

шовини́ст "shuh vyee NYEEST" 'chauvinist'

One of the peculiarities of *sha* is that ша and шо in unaccented syllables are sometimes pronounced as though ше or ши were written. This is represented by "shi" in the first two examples above. It occurs especially in a few native Russian words, and optionally (as an acceptable but not required pronunciation) elsewhere. It is least likely to be heard in words borrowed from Western European languages like most of those in the list here.

In шашлык, the pronunciation with "shi" is closer to the origianl than the pronunciation with "shah", for Russian got this word from one of the Tatar languages in which it occurs as *shishlik* or *shyshlyk*.

Ж ("ZHE"): ZH

30

24.1

ж = zh	Ж = Zh

жанр "ZHAHNR" 'genre'

Жу́ков "ZHOO kuhf" 'Zhukov'

Жда́нов "ZHDAH nuhf" 'Zhdanov'

журна́л "zhoor NAHL" 'journal'

пижа́ма "pyee ZHAH muh" 'pyjama'

буржу́й "boor ZHOOY" 'bourgeois'

ло́жа "LAW zhuh" 'loge'

Ни́жний Но́вгород "NYEE zhnyee NAWV guh ruht"
'Nizhni Novgorod'

Max Eastman wrote a long time ago: "The Russians have a great, fat, double-squatting letter that looks like a toad sitting on his grandmother and making pious motions with his arms."

Could he have been describing any letter but this one? Sometimes in Russian primers a picture of a toad enlivens the page on which ж is introduced, for 'toad' in Russian is жа́ба "ZHAH buh".

The letter is called *zhe* ("ZHE"). It is transliterated as *zh*, a pure convention because although we have the sound in English we have no fixed or unambiguous way of writing it. We represent it by *s* in *measure*, by *z* in *azure*, and by *g* in *rouge*.

What we find unusual about the Russian "zh" sound is that it often occurs at the beginning of a word. We find it hard in that position because that is contrary to our speech habits.

24.2

жест "ZHEST" 'gesture'

желе́ "zhi LYE" 'jelly'

желати́н "zhi lah TYEEN" 'gelatin'

сюже́т "syoo ZHET" 'subject' (French *sujet*)

дирижёр "dyee ryee ZHAWR" 'conductor' (coined in Russian from French *diriger* 'to conduct')

мужи́к "moo ZHEEK" 'muzhik'

режи́м "ryi ZHEEM" 'regime'

пассажи́р "puh sah ZHEER" 'passenger'

Нижи́нский "nyee ZHEEN ski" 'Nijinsky'

жира́ф "zhi RAHF" 'giraffe'

Жива́го "zhi VAH guh" 'Zhivago'

Ж behaves very much like ш. There is a soft "zh" sound, but it is limited to very special circumstances in a small number of words. For our immediate purposes we may say that the sound represented by ж is always hard. же and жё are simply "ZHE" and "ZHAW", without any "y" effect. жи is pronounced as though it were written жы; the "EE" in "moo ZHEEK" is the dull "ee" that was discussed for ы in section 22.1.

24.3

жаке́т "zhi KYET" 'jacket'

жарго́н "zhahr GAWN" 'jargon'

жанда́рм "zhahn DAHRM" 'gendarme'

жоке́й "zhah KYEI" 'jockey'

жонглёр "zhahn GLYAWR" 'juggler' (French *jongleur*)

жасми́н "zhah SMYEEN" 'jasmine'

жалюзи́ "zhah lyoo ZYEE" 'venetian blind'

These examples show further similarity of ж and ш.

Unaccented жа is sometimes pronounced "zhi" in a few words, represented here by жакет. More often, however, both жа and жо are pronounced with the same vowel sound as when а or о follows any other hard consonant.

24.4

гара́ж "gah RAHSH" 'garage'

бага́ж "bah GAHSH" 'baggage'

фура́ж "foo RAHSH" 'forage'

фюзеля́ж "fyoo zyi LYAHSH" 'fuselage'

мане́ж "mah NYESH" 'manege'

Воро́неж "vah RAW nyish" 'Voronezh'

When "zh" loses its voicing it becomes "sh". This happens at the end of a word: Russians don't say the "zh" sound in one of the positions where we find it very easy.

24.5

дро́жки "DRAW shkyi" 'droshky'

пирожки́ "pyi rah SHKYEE" 'pirozhki'

фура́жка "foo RAH shkuh" 'forage cap'

Даргомы́жский "duhr gah MWEESH ski" 'Dargomijsky'

Ж also represents a "sh" sound when it is written before a voiceless consonant.

24.6

джут "JOOT" 'jute'

Джонс "JAWNS" 'Jones'

джаз "JAHS" 'jazz'

джу́нгли "JOON glyi" 'jungle'

бюдже́т "byoo JET" 'budget'

пиджа́к "pyee JAHK" 'coat' (from *pea jacket*)

таджи́к "tah JEEK" 'Tajik'

Азербайджа́н "ah zyir bai JAHN" 'Azerbaijan'

бри́джи "BRYEE ji" 'breeches'

Russian has no letter for writing a "j" sound. In words taken from English and other languages, including many of the non-Russian languages of the Soviet Union, that have a "j" sound, Russian uses the combination дж *dzh*, as in the foregoing examples.

24.7

Джордж "JAWRCH" 'George'

бридж "BRYEECH" 'bridge'

колле́дж "kah LYECH" 'college'

The unvoicing of дж at the end of a word yields a "ch" sound rather than a "j".

Ц ("TSE"): TS

25.1

ц = ts	Ц = Ts

царе́вна "tsah RYE vnuh" 'tsarevna'

цари́ца "tsah RYEE tsuh" 'tsaritsa'

кварц "KVAHRTS" 'quartz'

Кузне́цк "koo ZNYETSK" 'Kuznetsk'

Кузнецо́в "koo znyi TSAWF" 'Kuznetsov'

Ц (*tse* "TSE") represents a compound sound, a "t" followed closely in the same articulation by an "s". It is thus quite like the German *z*, which also spells a "ts" combination. A German word *Quarz* is the original of both our *quartz* and the Russian кварц.

25.2

цент "TSENT" 'cent'

це́нзор "TSEN zuhr" 'censor'

цирк "TSEERK" 'circus'

медици́на "myi dyee TSEE nuh" 'medicine'

цеме́нт "tsi MYENT" 'cement'

цинк "TSEEN|K" 'zinc'

цисте́рна "tsi STYER nuh" 'cistern'

цыга́н "tsi GAHN" 'Gypsy'

Цари́цын "tsah RYEE tsin" 'Tasaritsyn'

Just as with ж, ц is a letter that always represents a hard consonant. There is no soft "ts" even when ц is followed by е or и. And the "ee" vowel after ц is the dull "ee" discussed in section 22.1, no matter whether цы or ци is written.

Цент 'cent', цирк 'circus', and other examples in this section show that the Russian "ts" often corresponds to our "s", written *c*. These represent different developments from the Latin *c*. Our "s" follows the pronunciation of the corresponding words in French. Russian follows the pronunciation in German. German these days uses *z* in words such as *Zement* and *Zirkus*, but they were once written with *c*'s: *Cement*, *Circus*.

цивилиза́ция "tsi vyi lyi ZAH tsi yuh" 'civilization'

церемо́ния "tsi ryi MAW nyi yuh" 'ceremony'

Цицеро́н "tsi tsi RAWN" 'Cicero'

цили́ндр "tsi LYEENDR" 'cylinder'

ци́фра "TSEE fruh" 'cipher'

юсти́ция "yoo STYEE tsi yuh" 'justice'

ака́ция "ah KAH tsi yuh" 'acacia'

конце́рт "kahn TSERT" 'concert'

офице́р "ah fyee TSER" 'officer'

проце́сс "prah TSES" 'process'

сце́на "STSE nuh" 'scene' 'stage'

Some further miscellaneous examples of ц:

Ге́рцен "GYER tsin" 'Herzen'

духобо́рцы "doo khah BAWR tsi" 'Dukhobors'

по́ловцы "PAW luhf tsi" 'Polovtsy (Polovetsians)'

пози́ция "pah ZYEE tsi yuh" 'position'

Румя́нцев "roo MYAHN tsif" 'Rumyantsev'

Суэ́ц "soo ETS" 'Suez'

Суэ́цкий Кана́л "soo ETS ki kah NAHL" 'Suez Canal'

Ч ("CHE"): CH

26.1

ч = ch	Ч = Ch

чек "CHEK" 'check'

Че́хов "CHE khuhf" 'Chekhov'

Чебуты́кин "chi boo TEE kyin" 'Chebutykin'

Чи́чиков "CHEE chi kuhf" 'Chichikov'

Со́чи "SAW chi" 'Sochi'

Чка́лов "CHKAH luhf" 'Chkalov'

Ни́ночка "NYEE nuh chkuh" 'Ninochka'

толка́ч "tahl KAHCH" 'tolkach (promoter)'

Шостако́вич "shuh stah KAW vyich" 'Shostakovich'

Ч is another letter that stands for a combination of sounds, but it gives us no particular difficulty because we have a traditional spelling for it in *ch*. The letter's name is *che* "CHE".

In neat contrast to the three letters that have just been indroduced (ш, ж, ц), ч represents a sound that is always *soft*. It begins with the tongue bunched in the front of the mouth as for a soft "t". It is not necessary, however, to put a "y" into the simulated pronunciations because our "ch" is a reasonable approximation.

Further examples:

Лобаче́вский "luh bah CHEF ski" 'Lobachevski'

черво́нец "chir VAW nyits" 'chervonets'

чернозём "chir nah ZYAWM" 'chernozem'

Вячесла́в "vyi chi SLAHF" 'Vyacheslav'

Соро́чинск "sah RAW chinsk" 'Sorochinsk'

аппара́тчик "ah pah RAHT chik" 'apparatchik'

попу́тчики "pah POOT chi kyee" 'poputchiki (fellow travelers)'

Петро́вич "pyi TRAW vyich" 'Petrovich'

царе́вич "tsah RYEI vyich" 'tsarevich'

Юде́нич "yoo DYEI nyich" 'Yudenich'

26.2

Пугачёв "poo gah CHAWF" 'Pugachëv, Pugachov'

Печо́ра "pyi CHAW ruh" 'Pechora'

да́ча "DAH chuh" 'dacha'

Колча́к "kahl CHAHK" 'Kolchak'

Камча́тка "kahm CHAHT kuh" 'Kamchatka'

каучу́к "kuh oo CHOOK" 'caouchouc, rubber'

Because ч is always a soft consonant, Russian writes ча and чу rather than чя and чю. Also, "CHAW" represents what is written чё in some situations and чо in others. The sounds are the same in either case.

Чапа́ев "chi PAH yif" 'Chapayev'

Гончаро́в "guhn chi RAWF" 'Goncharov'

Чайко́вский "chee KAWF ski" 'Tchaikovsky'

The status of ч as a perpetually soft consonant means that an a after it in an unaccented syllable is like я after other soft consonants (section 20.4): roughly like our "short i". The diphthong ай in this position is much like our "ee", as in the first represented pronunciation of Чайковский above; "chai KAWF-ski" is another common pronunciation that follows the spelling more closely.

LESSON TWENTY-SEVEN

Щ ("SHCHAH"): SHCH

27.1

щ = shch	Щ = Shch

щи "SHCHEE" 'shchi, stchi, shtchee' (cabbage soup)

борщ "BAWRSHCH" 'borsht, borsch, borscht, bortch'

това́рищ "tah VAH ryishch" 'tovarisch, tovarich'

Хрущёв "khroo SHCHAWF" 'Khrushchev'

Щ gives us foreigners a lot of trouble. You can see that reflected in the multiplicity and vagueness of the spellings of words that contain it when they pass into other languages.

It represents a sound sequence for which there are two pronunciations that the Russians accept as standard. One is a double or prolonged "sh", much like what you hear in the middle of *fresh sheets* except that the Russian "shsh" is all in one syllable, not split in the middle. In the other pronunciation there is a small movement of the tongue that turns the sequence into "shch", like what you hear in *fish chips* except that here again the sound is a continuous utterance, not divided between two syllables. This "shch" is easier to demonstrate and is the one used in transliteration and in identifying *shcha* by comparison with the sounds of other languages.

In either case, the sound is always soft, made with the tongue bunched in the front of the mouth (section 7.3). In this respect щ is like ч. It is not necessary to indicate softness by using я or ю in the Russian orthography, or by writing "y" in the approximated pronunciations. The sound of "SHCHAW" is the same whether spelled щё or що.

This pecular Russian letter originated in Old Slavic, where its sound was "sht". It was apparently a *sha* Ш written over a *te* Т, for in the earliest forms the tail was under the middle of the letter. It got the value of "shch" in Russian because of a difference between the systems of sounds in Old Slavic and Russian. The form of the letter changed under the hands of the Russian manuscript writers as the little tail migrated toward the right side where it is in the modern letter.

Here are some more examples:

Щедри́н "shchi DRYEEN" 'Shchedrin'

Щелка́лов "shchil KAH luhf" 'Shchelkalov, Stchelkalov'

Плеще́ев "plyi SHCHEI yif" 'Pleshcheyev'

Хова́нщина "khah VAHN shchi nuh" 'Khovanshchina, Khovanchina'

Зо́щенко "ZAW shchin kuh" 'Zoshchenko'

Благове́щенск "bluh gah VYEI shchinsk" 'Blagoveshchensk'

Ради́щев "rah DYEE shchif" 'Radishchev'

Голени́щев "guh lyi NYEE shchif" 'Golenishchev'

щепа́ "shchi PAH" 'chips'

я́щик "YAH shchik" 'box'

ь: (') THE SOFT SIGN

28.1

ро́ли "RAW lyee" 'roles'

роль "RAWL(Y)" 'role'

сте́пи "STYEI pyee" 'steppes'

степь "STYEIP(Y)" 'steppe'

цари́ "tsah RYEE" 'tsars'

царь "TSAHR(Y)" 'tsar'

шест "SHEST" 'pole'

шесть "SHEST(Y)" 'six'

Such things as "RAWL(Y)" are meaningless or misleading if you have to depend upon responses based on English letters and sounds. I am hoping that by now you have acquired enough familiarity with Russian soft consonants that you will realize that "RAWL(Y)" represents what is left when the final vowel is taken away from "RAW lyee" and we are left with a word ending in soft "l".

The soft consonants can and do occur at the end of a word. The letter ь is a device for indicating (when there is no following vowel letter to do so) that the consonant is soft. The Russians call it мягкий знак "MYAHKH ki znahk" 'the soft sign.'

In transliteration we often write an apostrophe (') in place of the soft sign. This is an arbitrary convention that is sometimes followed in technical works. In most contexts, an apostrophe at the end of names such as *Kazan'* and *Gogol'* is meaningless and it simply drops off: *Kazan*, *Gogol*.

In the simulated pronunciations, "(Y)" or "(y)" is not supposed to suggest a vowel or an additional syllable. It is supposed to indicate the softness (the "y" mixture) of the consonant before it.

Here are some futher examples:

Каза́нь "kah ZAHN(Y)" 'Kazan'

ию́нь "ee YOON(Y)" 'June'

ию́ль "ee YOOL(Y)" 'July'

арте́ль "ahr TYEIL(Y)" 'artel'

ру́бль "ROOBL(Y)" 'ruble'

Кре́мль "KRYEML(Y)" 'Kremlin'

Го́голь "GAW guhl(y)" 'Gogol'

со́боль "SAW buhl(y)" 'sable'

алта́рь "ahl TAHR(Y)" 'altar'

Сиби́рь "syee BYEER(Y)" 'Siberia'

И́горь "EE guhr(y)" 'Igor'

Обь "AWP(Y)" 'Ob'

Любо́вь "lyoo BAWF(Y)" 'Liubov'

28.2

О́льга "AWL(Y) guh" 'Olga'

Го́рький "GAWR(Y) ki" 'Gorki'

Ха́рьков "KHAHR(Y) kuhf" 'Kharkov'

Тара́с Бу́льба "tah RAHS BOOL(Y) buh" 'Taras Bulba'

Большо́й "bahl(y) SHOI" 'Bolshoy'

большеви́к "buhl(y) shi VYEEK" 'Bolshevik'

The soft sign also occurs inside a word, between consonants, as these examples show. It is usually an indicator of a soft consonant that is followed by a hard one. Under some circumstances it may also stand between two soft consonants, as in:

Ильмень "EEL(Y) myin(y)" 'Ilmen'

Раскольников "rah SKAWL(Y) nyi kuhf" 'Raskolnikov'

28.3

An *l* in a word borrowed from a Western European language is likely to turn up in Russian as a soft "l". (This has already been noted in section 20.3). That is why you find the soft sign at the end of words such as:

сти́ль "STYEEL(Y)" 'style'

дуэ́ль "doo EL(Y)" 'duel'

карусе́ль "kuh roo SYEIL(Y)" 'carrousel'

автомоби́ль "ah ftuh mah BYEEL(Y)" 'automobile'

and between л and another consonant in words like these:

альбо́м "ahl(y) BAWM" 'album'

А́льпы "AHL(Y) pwi" 'Alps'

бульва́р "bool(y) VAHR" 'boulevard'

бульдо́зер "bool(y) DAW zyir" 'bulldozer'

культу́ра "kool(y) TOO ruh" 'culture'

пу́льс "POOL(Y)S" 'pulse'

та́льк "TAHL(Y)K" 'talc'

фи́льм "FYEEL(Y)M" 'film'

Another important point about the function of the soft sign can be approached through the contrast of syllables such as those underlined in the two pairs of words that follow:

Ля́дов "LYAH duhf" 'Liadov'

Илья́ "ee L(Y)YAH" 'Ilya'

тя́нут "TYAH noot" '(they) pull'

Татья́на "tah T(Y)YAH nuh" 'Tatiana'

This is subtle and likely to be hard.

ля "LYAH" is a soft "l" followed by the vowel "ah".

лья "L(Y)YAH" is a soft "l" followed by "yah".

тя "TYAH" is a soft "t" followed by the vowel "ah".

тья "T(Y)YAH" is a soft "t" followed by "yah".

The soft sign shows that the consonant before it is soft, and a я after it has the same value as at the beginning of a word or after a vowel, that is, "yah".

After the soft sign, similarly, е stands for "yeh", ё stands for "yaw", and ю stands for "yoo".

These contrasts are one of the reasons for insisting from the first mention of soft consonants (section 7.3) that such a sequence as нет contains three sounds "ny-e-t" rather than four; if there were a full "y" sound here, Russian would write ньет.

Here are some further examples in Russian names:

Ната́лья "nah TAH l(y)yuh" 'Natalya'

Улья́нов "oo L(Y)YAH nuhf" 'Ulyanov'

Со́фья "SAW f(y)yuh" 'Sofya'

Проко́фьев "prah KAW f(y)yif" 'Prokofieff'

Игна́тьев "ee GNAH t(y)yif" 'Ignatiev'

Афана́сьев "ah fah NAH s(y)yif" 'Afanasiev'

Соловьёв "suh lah V(Y)YAWF" 'Soloviëv, Solovyoff'

Муравьёв "moo rah V(Y)YAWF" 'Muraviëv'

Ильюшин "ee L(Y)YOO shin" 'Ilyushin'

Here are some miscellaneous examples in words of foreign origin:

коньяк "kah N(Y)YAHK" 'cognac'

Пьер "P(Y)YER" 'Pierre'

пьеса "P(Y)YE suh" 'play' (French *pièce*)

карьера "kah R(Y)YE ruh" 'career'

Ньютон "N(Y)YOO tuhn" 'Newton'

Нью Йорк "N(Y)YOO YAWRK" 'New York'

In borrowed words, a soft sign and a following "YAW" are written sometimes ьё, sometimes ьо:

серьёзный "syi R(Y)YAW zni" 'serious' (French *sérieux*)

бульон "boo L(Y)YAWN" 'bouillon'

компаньон "kuhm pah N(Y)YAWN" 'companion'

фьорд "F(Y)YAWRT" 'fjord'

28.5

After the soft sign, и represents "yee" and may be transliterated *yi*. A familiar example is in a name you have undoubtedly seen:

Ильич "ee L(Y)YEECH" 'Ilyich'

Some other names in which it appears are:

Ильин "ee L(Y)YEEN" 'Ilyin'

Ильинский "ee L(Y)YEEN ski" 'Ilyinski'

Ильичёв "ee l(y)yee CHAWF" 'Ilyichëv'

28.6

A final note about the uses of the soft sign.

You have seen that the sounds represented by ш *sha* and ж *zhe* are always (with minor exceptions) hard, and those spelled by ч *che* and щ *shcha* are always soft. A soft sign has no effect on the sounds represented by any of these letters. Nevertheless, it does occur after all of them.

At the end of a word, the soft sign may have grammatical significance. For instance, the soft sign at the end of ночь "NAWCH" 'night' shows that this is grammatically a feminine noun, while луч "LOOCH" 'ray', is a masculine noun.

Inside a word, the soft sign shows that there is a full "y" sound before the following vowel. An example is in the geographic name Запоро́жье "zuh pah RAW zhyuh" 'Zaporozhye'. The last syllable of that name is not the same as the last syllable of ложе "LAW zhuh" 'couch'.

ъ: (") THE HARD SIGN

29.1

This is another letter than represents no sound of its own.

You might have expected it after discovering that Russian has a "soft sign." This is the "hard sign" and that is exactly what its Russian name means: твёрдый знак "TVYAWR di znahk". We transliterate it arbitrarily by a double apostrophe (") in order to contrast it with the soft sign(').

The range of its use is nothing like as great as that of the soft sign. At the end of a word and often inside a word a hard consonant needs no marker. The mere absence of a soft sign shows that the л in канал "kah NAHL" 'canal' and Волга "VAWL guh", for instance, is a hard "l".

The hard sign is written between a consonant and a letter such as ю, е, я, or и in situations where the history of the word suggests that the consonant should be hard. Spelling is more conservative than speech, however. Sometimes the consonant actually is soft; but there is some fluctuation in these pronunciations, and at any rate the spelling remains true to the word history.

One of these situations is in borrowed words. In the following examples the "y" sound reflects the pronunciation of *j* in German and in Latin:

адъюта́нт "ah d(y)yoo TAHNT" 'adjutant'

конъекту́ра "kuh n(y)yik TOO ruh" 'conjecture'

конъюнкту́ра "kuh n(y)yoon|k TOO ruh" 'conjuncture'

объе́кт "ah BYEKT" 'object'

субъе́кт "soo BYEKT" 'subject'

29.2

For this concluding note I have to cite a few Russian words that have no resemblance to anything you may have seen, for they aren't names and they aren't of the sort that we borrow from Russian.

They are words beginning with prefixes that function in much the same way that *con-*, *ex-*, *sub-*, and the like do in many English words.

When a prefix ending in a consonant comes before a stem that begins with a "y" sound, the hard sign is written as a separator. Here again the spelling is true to the history of these words, but in modern times the consonant often is soft.

The word for 'exemption' contains a prefix из- that corresponds to *ex-*; the rest of the word is -ятие, corresponding to *-emption* (in Russian and in English an exemption is a "taking out"); but the word is written thus:

изъя́тие "ee Z(Y)YAH tyi yuh"

Similarly, in съезд "S(Y)YEST" 'congress' the prefix is с- 'con-', the hard sign is a separator, and the stem is -езд '-gress' (in both languages, a congress is a "coming together").

APPENDICES

SOME NEW WORDS FOR YOU TO PRACTICE

The words listed here are often rather obvious equivalents of English forms. They are given without pronunciations or glosses so that you can test yourself on the preceding lessons. Use the table of Russian letters if you need a reminder of the sounds. You may want to try your hand at transliteration, too.

автотури́ст
аэрозо́ль
атлети́зм
антиамерикани́зм

бадминто́н
бестсе́ллер
био́ник
букле́т

видеотелефо́н

га́мма-глобули́н
гелиоэнерге́тика
геофи́зик
глоба́льный
голографи́я

дакро́н
джип
джудо́
ди́зель-электри́ческий

зоопланкто́н

интерпо́л
интеллектуа́л
инфраструкту́ра
йогу́рт

кинодокуме́нт
кинокри́тик
кинопродю́сер
ко́ка-ко́ла
конформи́зм
кортизо́н
конфронта́ция

ла́зер
ла́зерный
ЛСД

марихуа́на
ма́фия
микроминиатюриза́ция
микрофи́льм
минискёрт

ЮПИ (=UPI)

эскала́ция
электроэнцефалогра́мма
электро́ник

моде́ль
моте́ль
мю́зикл

непрофессиона́л
неоколониали́зм
нейтри́но
номенклату́ра

океана́вт

пабли́сити
пла́зма
плейбо́й
подпрогра́мма

радиоастроно́м
репортёр
ре́слер
рок-н-ро́лл

секс
сёрфинг
синте́тика
смог
стресс
стрипти́з
стрипти́зка

транзи́стор
телеинтервью́
телекоммента́тор
термопла́стика
тефло́н
турбомаши́на

уикэ́нд

фибергла́с
фотожурнали́ст

хо́бби
хобби́ст

цуна́ми

ча-ча-ча́

шед

экспериме́нт

KEY TO PRONUNCIATION

CONSONANTS

symbol	*as in English*
B b	*b*in
D d	*d*in (p. 6, 46)
F f	*f*in
G g	*g*ot
K k	*k*in
L l	*l*ot (p. 49)
M m	*m*at
N n	*n*ot (p. 16)
P p	*p*in (p. 52)
R r	*r*ot (p. 7)
S s	*s*in
T t	*t*in
V v	*v*at
Z z	*z*ig-*z*ag
KH kh	(no equivalent: p. 34)
TS ts	si*ts*
CH ch	*ch*ew
SH sh	*sh*oot
SHCH shch	fi*sh ch*ips (p. 83)
ZH zh	*z* in azure
Y y	*y*aw
(Y) (y)	(no equivalent: p. 20)
W w	*w*et (p. 68)

VOWELS

symbol	*as in English*
Ah ah	f*a*ther
AW aw	h*aw*k
AI ai	*ai*sle
E e	b*e*t
EE ee	b*ee*t
EI ei	*ei*ght
I i	b*i*t
OO oo	b*oo*t
OOY ooy	b*uoy*
OI oi	b*oi*l
uh	meth*o*d and sof*a*

STRESS

The syllable in a word with the principal accent is shown in all capital letters:

СОВЕ́Т "sah VYET"

n|k The | is used to remind you that *n* is never the *n* in *sink* and *singular*.

CHART OF THE LETTERS

YOU KNOW THESE	THESE MAY FOOL YOU	THESE ARE NEW	ENGLISH EQUIVALENT	AMERICAN PRONUNCIATION*	LESSON NUMBER
А а			A a	ah, uh	2.2
		Б б	B b	b	19
	В в		V v	v	4
		Г г	G g	g	14
		Д д	D d	d	15
	Е е		Ye, ye	ye, yi	7
	Ё ё		Yo, yo	yaw	8
		Ж ж	Zh, zh	zh	24
		З з	Z z	z	12
		И и	I i	ee, i	9
		Й й	I i	i, y	2.5
К к			K k	k	2.2
		Л л	L l	l	16
М м			M m	m	3
	Н н		N n	n	5
О о			O o	aw, ah, uh	2.3
		П п	P p	p	17
	Р р		R r	r	2.4
	С с		S s	s	6
Т т			T t	t	2.2
	У у		U u	oo	10
		Ф ф	F f	f	18
	Х х		Kh, kh	kh	11
		Ц ц	Ts, ts	ts	25
		Ч ч	Ch, ch	ch	26
		Ш ш	Sh, sh	sh	23
		Щ щ	Shch, shch	shch	27
		ъ	(hard sign)		29
		ы	y	ee, i	22
		ь	(soft sign)	(y)	28
		Э э	E e	e	13
		Ю ю	Yu, yu	yoo	21
		Я я	Ya, ya	yah, yi	20

*Symbols in stressed syllables are rendered in all capital form.

RUSSIAN WRITING

А а	А	а
Б б	Б	б, б
В в	В	в
Г г	Г	г
Д д	Д	д, д
Е е	Е	е
Ё ё	Ё	ё
Ж ж	Ж	ж
З з	З	з
И и	И	и
Й й	Й	й
К к	К	к
Л л	Л	л
М м	М	м
Н н	Н, Н	н
О о	О	о

П п	П, п	п
Р р	Р	р, р
С с	С	с
Т т	Т	т, т̄, т
У у	У	у
Ф ф	Ф, Ф	ф
Х х	Х	х
Ц ц	Ц	ц
Ч ч	Ч	ч
Ш ш	Ш	ш, ш̲
Щ щ	Щ	щ
ъ		ъ
ы		ы
ь		ь, ь
Э э	Э	э
Ю ю	Ю, Ю	ю
Я я	Я	я